Working and Writing for Change

Working and Writing for Change

Series Editors: Steve Parks and Jessica Pauszek

The Working and Writing for Change series began during the 100th anniversary celebrations of NCTE. It was designed to recognize the collective work of teachers of English, Writing, Composition, and Rhetoric to work within and across diverse identities to ensure the field recognize and respect language, educational, political, and social rights of all students, teachers, and community members. While initially solely focused on the work of NCTE/CCCC Special Interest Groups and Caucuses, the series now includes texts written by individuals in partnership with other communities struggling for social recognition and justice.

Books in the Series

CCCC/NCTE Caucuses

Viva Nuestro Caucus: Rewriting the Forgotten Pages of Our Caucus ed. by Romeo García, Iris D. Ruiz, Anita Hernández & María Paz Carvajal Regidor

History of the Black Caucus National Council Teachers of English by Marianna White Davis

Listening to Our Elders: Working and Writing for Social Change by Samantha Blackmon, Cristina Kirklighter, & Steve Parks

Building a Community, Having a Home: A History of the Conference on College Composition and Communication ed. by Jennifer Sano-Franchini, Terese Guinsatao Monberg, & K. Hyoejin Yoon

Community Publications

The People Demand Democracy: Voices from the Myanmar Spring Revolution, edited by Pratha Purushottam, et al.

A Parent's POWER by Sylvia P. Simms

The Forever Colony by Victor Villanueva

Visibly (and Invisibly) Muslin on Grounds: Classroom, Culture, and Community at the University of Virginia, ed. by Wafa Salah and Fawzia Tahsin

The Lived Experience of Democracy: Criticizing Injustice, Building Community, ed. by Kaitlyn Baker, et al.

Steal the Street: The Intersection of Homelessness and Gentrification by Mark Mussman

Literacy and Pedagogy in an Age of Misinformation and Disinformation ed. by Tara Lockhart, Brenda Glascott, Chris Warnick, Juli Parrish, & Justin Lewis

Faces of Courage: Ten Years of Building Sanctuary by Harvey Finkle

Equality and Justice: An Engaged Generation, a Troubled World by Michael Chehade, Alex Granner, Ahmed Abdelhakim Hachelaf, Madhu Napa, Samantha Owens, & Steve Parks

Other People's English: Code-Meshing, Code-Switching, and African American Literacy by Vershawn Ashanti Young, Rusty Barrett, Y'Shanda Young-Rivera, & Kim Brian Lovejoy

Becoming International: Musings on Studying Abroad in America, ed. by Sadie Shorr-Parks

Dreams and Nightmares: I Fled Alone to the United States When I Was Fourteen by Liliana Velásquez. ed. and trans. by Mark Lyon

The Weight of My Armor: Creative Nonfiction and Poetry by the Syracuse Veterans' Writing Group, ed. by Ivy Kleinbart, Peter McShane, & Eileen Schell

PHD to PhD: How Education Saved My Life by Elaine Richardson

The Forever Colony

Victor Villanueva

Parlor Press
Anderson, South Carolina
www.parlorpress.com

Parlor Press LLC, Anderson, South Carolina, USA
Copyright © 2024 by Victor Villanueva.

Library of Congress Cataloging-in-Publication Data on File

1 2 3 4 5

978-1-64317-473-0 (paperback)
978-1-64317-474-7 (PDF)

Working and Writing for Change
An Imprint Series of Parlor Press
Series Editors: Steve Parks and Jessica Pauszek

Interior design by Justin Lewis // justinlewis.me

Parlor Press, LLC is an independent publisher of scholarly and trade titles in print and multimedia formats. This book is available in paper and eBook formats from Parlor Press on the World Wide Web at www.parlorpress.com or through online and brick-and-mortar bookstores. For submission information or to find out about Parlor Press publications, write to Parlor Press, 3015 Brackenberry Drive, Anderson, South Carolina, 29621, or email editor@parlorpress.com.

Contents

for Stela

Acknowledgments

First, my thanks to Steve Parks for considering then accepting this genre bender, for allowing me to enter Burke's never-ending conversation of the Parlor [Press] in the *Working and Writing for Change* series. This is where I wanted this little book to appear.

Thanks, of course, to the reviewers, anonymous and signed, who told me what I needed to consider and reconsider, making for what I hope is a somewhat better text. And then there are the friends and kin who took the time to look at and comment on some of my earlier flailings: my daughter AnaSofía, Brother Bob, Elitza, Mitzi, Victor Unda, and especially my friend, guide, partner, spouse, Rochelle. And even if they hadn't read my flailings, would any of this had been possible or would any of it had mattered if I hadn't had the company of my daughters and son—Steven, Serena, Alma, AnaSofía, and Sonia?

I've always loved the idea of Burke's Parlor. But in my home, the hub has been the kitchen rather than the parlor. It was around The Kitchen Table that so many conversations have taken place, from childhood to just the other day, and not just the literal table of the kitchen but the symbolic kitchen table of the seminar room, with all those conversations with graduate students who both listened and who prodded in the spirit of Chantal Mouffe's *agonism*.

To all of you: family, friends, and students, I couldn't thank you more for being—in that special sense of *being*—with me.

A Preface and Prologue

¿De dónde eres? *(Where are you from?)*

I had just started to settle into my seat on a flight from Costa Rica. The older gentleman in the next seat over stares at my boarding pass and U.S. passport—"Villanueva, Victor." His curiosity obviously killing him, he asks "¿De dónde eres?" I say, "Soy de Nueva York, pero mi' padres son de Puerto Rico." I am from New York, but my parents are from Puerto Rico. It is who I am. It is how I see.

There is a memory, a mythical memory maybe, of Puerto Rico, or of being Puerto Rican that was formed by the stories told by Mom and Dad while they were with us; stories from the tenants of the old neighborhood, folks who came from different parts of the Island. And there is the memory born in a language, the dialect, the particular ways with words and pronunciations that reflect a location and a history. For me, simply saying "Spanish" doesn't quite do the trick, a matter I know from blank expressions when speaking to other Latines.[1] There was a character on some TV show or other who was supposed to be from one of the Central American countries, but when he spoke Spanish, it sounded so much like my own Spanish that I had to look up the actor on Google. He was a Puerto Rican from New York. I knew it, even though he didn't drop the final *-s* or drop the *-d* that is a part of the Puerto Rican dialect; I still heard it. And there have been other signs of difference within the language that is Spanish. There were the blank looks I got in Costa Rica when I asked where I might find *la bodega* ("Ah," I'm told after I explained that I was looking to buy food and the like, "*¡el supermercado!*"). Or the time one of my daughters ordered *habichuelas* during her visit to Cuba only to get green beans rather than the black beans she was expecting. She had learned that red beans were PR and black beans were Cuban (not quite true, but when I made black beans at home I called them "Cuban beans"). For us, beans are *habichuelas* (even the green beans, which are *habichuelas nuevas*). At least that's how I was taught. And when I first went to a Mexican restaurant (long, long ago now), I was troubled to see *puerco*, pig, on the menu rather than *pernil* or *cerdo*, pork. Or there was my surprise in learning that *pasteles* means cakes or pastries for most and not the special meal Mom and Dad and I would make during Christmas: *cerdo* encased in plantain dough (*masa de platanos*), wrapped in banana husks or paper and boiled. And on and on: *mofongo,* another plantain delicacy; or *chinas* or *guineos* for breakfast; or running to catch *la guagua* to get to school on time. My point is that even as I am a "heritage speaker" (English dominant, not fully bilingual, yet not at all monolingual), mine is the Spanish of Puerto Rico through Brooklyn, even after so many decades living in the West, the Southwest, and the Pacific Northwest (most of my life, as it turns out), though all of *those* Spanishes did work their ways into mine (which would always aggravate my mother).

But there's more than foods that are a part of being, of course. I'm thinking here of the reflections of faith among the families of my Brooklyn neighborhoods and from Mom and Dad. Mom was raised in the Church, almost literally, raised in the rectory of the parish priest in Río Piedras, where the woman who raised her, the one she called *Mami*, was the housekeeper. Dad was raised in some mix of *espiritismo, sanse, y Católico*, his mother a medium or channeler, a rosary carefully wrapped around her fist or draped over a glass of holy water on the Mesa Blanca, the household alter.

Memories and tales of the Island.

Rochelle and I were talking about current politics, the spring of 2023, and she says that her father was a die-hard Democrat while her mother was a Republican, yet they never argued, simply saw things differently. And that got me thinking of my own parents. I just assumed they were Democrats, but I really don't remember any talk of Democrats or Republicans. Dad would quietly "tsk" at the mess being made by the

Puerto Rican governor, Muñoz Marín, and his Operation Bootstrap, or Dad would chuckle at the failed U.S. attempts at getting Fidel Castro. Mom would simply scowl softly; none of that mattered.

1955 or 1956. An afternoon in Washington Square, our having taken the subway from Brooklyn. Washington Square and Greenwich Village on sunny spring days, the cleanliness and the sense of peace. On one of those quiet afternoons in Washington Square, Dad left Mom to her novela on a park bench while he took me to one of those lovely brownstones by the park, the one with the "To Let" sign on the first-floor window.

Dad knocks, a man opens, and Dad asks about the apartment for rent. A kind seeming older fellow tells Dad that the place is no longer available. Dad shakes his head, squeezes my shoulder as if to say, "stay quiet and listen," then says that it's been hard to find a place since our coming from Spain. Hesitation from the landlord or super: "Well, why don't you come back after lunch. We might be able to work something out."

"Spain" was the speakeasy password. No entry for the "Portorican."

It's funny how some memories, no matter how long ago, remain crystal clear: the smells of Washington Square so different from the hallways of home, the heat of the sun on the trees that day, the voices, the words said, and the lesson learned.

Colonialism. Racism. Memories.

The tales to follow will reflect—like all tales do—particular ideological predispositions. There is, after all, a particular world view that comes from being a Brooklyn-born Puerto Rican, born at the end of the 1940s, recognizing the racism and its ties to coloniality, having known the urge to assimilate and never having been granted full entry, despite military service and all and even a PhD, thanks to great extent to those years in the military that made college a possibility: the concessions of hegemony. And when I became an academic and began to publish, my mind, my writing, could not but tell of racism and colonialism—from my first national publication, throughout what is now nearly a forty-year career.[2]

It was early in my career when I discovered Frantz Fanon and soon thereafter Enrique Dussel.[3] More recently came the discovery of the decolonial theorists beyond Dussel, though I would read them through the eyes of someone trained in U.S. rhetorical theory (especially Kenneth Burke) as well as the "classics,"[4] and through the eyes of someone who had long established a political-theoretical attachment to Antonio Gramsci and the Gramscian post-Marxists as well as the Gramsci-like theorists on social class and political economy (thinking here of Erik Olin Wright especially).[5] So rather than simply accept decolonial theorists' use of the term *rhetoric* and the epistemological, I read the decolonial as displayed through *epistemic rhetorics[6] of modernity, ideologically maintained through the common sense as displayed in common topics.*[7] Each of the chapters to follow is headed by what I see as a dominant commonplace, my turning to the convenience of the established *konoi topoi* of Ancient Greek or the locī commūnēs of Latin, the colonizer's conventions.[8]

All that said, what follows is not about the theory; it's about stories of the world's oldest colony.

What follows are my historical and imaginative journeys seen through a rhetorical lens—stories—and the ways the histories trigger thoughts on colonialism and racism as they might pertain to Puerto Rico and to my own internal colonialism.

The stories are told mainly by a spirit who is the memory of the Island and its people, *Bushika*. She describes her beginnings in the Amazon, the people's journey north, and what transpires on the Island—Colón and Ponce de León, but mainly others sometimes forgotten: the *cacica* (queen) Yuíza, the pirate Miguel Enríquez, the revolutionaries of the 19th century, tales told through the Spirit *Bushika* and other narrators, fictional characters, and their somewhat magical yet historical journeys.

At bottom, the stories to follow are allegories. Along the way, I have drawn from formal histories of Puerto Rico.[9] In other words, here is another set of stories, imaginings drawn from memories of my now-departed parents; the stories from my childhood family, friends, and neighbors; and the works of scholars. What follows is simply a somewhat fictional, somewhat historical, decidedly rhetorical journey with the spirit of Memory.

1 Bushika
metaphor [10]

We were looking at old family pictures while visiting Mom and Dad in the little apartment attached to the office of the motel they managed when we came across an old sepia photo of Dad's parents, my grandparents, don Basilio y Mama Pina, looking old, like those in their eighties or nineties might look today.

My girlfriend asks Dad, "So are you part Indian?" Mama Pina, especially, did look stereotypically American Indian. Mom grabs the picture with that look that could whither the sturdiest weed, saying "No" in that Spanish way that cuts the syllable in half. Dad just looks at me with an almost-a-smile and flips his eyebrows. Then, risking that look from Mom, he says while turning the corners of his mouth downward, shrugging, palms facing up, "Well, everybody has some Indian, no?" Didn't know if he was referring to Puerto Ricans or saying that indigeneity itself is global.

I am Bushika. I had lived among the Yanomami along the Orinoco River. And when I died, I left behind a son, Daví. He was my only child, the product less of a romance than a mating. My fate would not be to love a man but to love a People. I had the child and then was taken by the fever. And though the shaman Mukashe had grabbed the spirit of the fever within me, absorbed it into himself— old and frail as he was, held it until he felt it die within before spitting it out, he was too late; the damage had been done. So Daví

5

cremated my body and ate the ashes after mixing the ashes with manioc. This was our way, how I would be remembered, my name never again to be spoken among the living Yanomami.

And so my spirit rose up to the Record, the Record that contains the scenes of lives lived and lives yet to come.

I was surrounded in it all, immersed in the images and the sounds that had come before, those that passed, though only from the perspective of the future and the potentials of what might come after, what some would later call "history." The Record transcends the records of the scribes to come.

And here, immersed within the Record, I saw the First People cross over narrow passages in the faraway cold, those who came before and after the Great Cold, far from what would become the homes of the Yanomami. They traveled east over the foreign landscape and then south toward the warmth. And some would stay in the places of ice and snow, something I understood and could see but never experienced. And some would continue traveling through stiff, tall, green woods, through different kinds of green. And some would pass the woods to travel through the dry red rock and then pass the rock striped red and grey and purple. And some would continue further still, though some did stay in the spaces that looked to me like barren land. And the travelers continued over hundreds of thousands of turnings of the moon from dark to bright to dark and back again. And some settled where the rivers are plenty, the leaves are large and heavy with moisture and the weather warm, and where there is much to gather and to hunt. These are my people. Home.

I am awash in sound and sight, sounds not of my tongue but I somehow understood and understood to be connected to me and to my Daví. I somehow know that I am hearing the tongue to be called Arawakan, connected to the people of the Aruacay along the Orinoco. I know somehow. Somehow. All strange and familiar. And I remember the story of the many tongues I heard as a child, how there was a place of seven caves, each cave threaded with the blood of a god, so that the people of each of the caves came out speaking the language of their particular god of the cave.[11] Later, others would tell another version of the tale, changing in the way tales do when passed by storytellers such as me, at least until the time of writing that will begin with carvings on rock. And even then, different ones will say that the carvings say different things.

There will always be the storytellers, tellers of the line of the people. More of the men than the women would fight wars, and the warriors, too, would tell stories, even if only to bring peace, perhaps by way of the *wayamou*, a rhetoric for peace. But storytelling fell more to the women who knew best how to listen, who knew listening was no less an art than speaking. Such were my evenings before I left the soil: sitting before the *shabono*, the circular huts for all of the clan, its courtyard in the center, where we would speak and listen, telling stories and listening to stories of things past or to come or just the wonders of possibility or making one another laugh in the evening warmth.

But here, now, in this rush of visuals and of sounds of things past, things future-past, and the possibilities yet to come, I see and I hear, neither standing nor sitting nor floating, surrounded. And when I look down, I see my hands, still smooth. And when I touch my face, I still feel the stick-piercings along my cheeks and through my nose. And I know that I have not changed, even as I am no longer of the flesh.

Then I am pulled from my musing by the appearance of three women, each with a beauty like nothing I had ever before seen. And I know, somehow, that they, too, are mothers. One says she is Miryam, another says she is called Candelaria, and a third I know to be Atabey. They are without age. The Record is all beginnings and ends—or no beginnings and only possibilities.

Miryam stands before me, a white rough-looking mantle framing her light brown face, nearly a child, a face of pure peace and sorrow. She speaks to me in a faraway tongue, but I understand.

"Do not worry, Bushika. There is a fruitful and well-watered land, clear water, a rainforest you can enter and from which you can depart. A place for the People. It is different from the home you have known. When the People arrive at that place, they will be like Adam and Chava, the People able to discard their coverings of the body, living without shame for a time. You will point the way to Davi."

Then Candelaria speaks. While Miryam is dressed in simple white and blue, Candelaria's veil is lined in red, a dark blue with yellow, the yellow like the twinkling of stars, and there are red marks along the seam of the veil, marks that I do not yet understand. And in Candelaria's left hand is a candle, but where our candles are made from animal fat so that they are yellow, hers is white. Candelaria is darker than Miryam, nearly as dark as I see myself, yet her hair is the color of the *cupuaçu* fruit— not brown, not orange, not yellow, yet all of that. Another strange tongue yet clear to me.

"Study the record before you, Bushika. You will be Memory, appearing among our family, the line of mothers and daughters and sons."

Then Atabey. She feels familiar though I am not sure why. She is naked, sitting on her haunches like we do when giving birth. And she, too, is an unusual beauty. All she says is that "The People will come to know me and my sons, especially my son Yúcahu Vagu Maorocotí, the giver of manioc, *la yuca*, the root of life."

So it is that the Record will inform all that I will say to you. I am Bushika. I am the storyteller and memory of the birth and life of a people.

II

Daví has grown to a fine young man, thin but not frail, with thick, shiny black hair, shaved, like we do, below the line of a bowl; his black eyes sparkle, and he is given to a ready smile, especially since he still has all his teeth. He continues to know me from within. He had kept some of who I was in a hollowed gourd, ready to consume a finger's pinch at those moments when he begins to lose the memory of me, when he tries to see my face but finds himself unable, my face disappearing the harder he tries to see.

On a rainless wet day under the grand broad leaves of the forest, a day with plenty of meat and fruit, he felt the need for a journey, for his spirit to wander.

"Ah, Hekura, I have an urge to speak to the spirits this day. The time is right, I feel."

Hekura is my brother, uncle to Daví, the one Daví will live with when there comes a time that a woman chooses him for a mate. Hekura is much older than Daví. It shows in the lines of Hekura's face, the thinness of his thighs, the protrusion of his belly. But like Daví, Hekura is good-natured, always willing to please. So Hekura helps the young Daví begin a short journey of the soul, holding the long sacred pipe while Daví places the tapered tip into his nostril and sucks in the *yâkoana* that Hekura has blown through the pipe.

Daví takes in as much as he can, sneezing out the rest, rubbing his nose and face as he walks away. He returns to squat before Hekura for a spell. Then Daví jumps up, dances and sings and giggles. "And maybe I will speak with my *Naya*," he says aloud to no one in particular. I am pleased that he still calls me *naya*, like the little ones do of their mothers, but he is much more interested in having the women look at his dancing and his good spirits as he sings. Maybe one will choose him. And he grows excited at the possibilities. They're looking, he knows. Some are thinking him a fool; others interested. But as he turns to look at the women in the *shabono*, I must appear. Daví shuts his eyes. "Not now, please, *Naya*," he whispers to me. But mothers are mothers, whether alive or dead. So I must block his view of the young women in their hammocks.

"Not now," he says again, more loudly. "I am much more interested in my future than the past, *Naya*, please."

"I, too, am interested in the future, Daví. You have work to do. You must become fully a man, a speaker of peace and possibility. You must speak to the people of the land. Speak to the other villages of the Yanomami; make peace with all of those of the river, with Ye'Kuana; De'áruwa, Híwi, E'ñepa, the Hodi. Speak to Krihisiwa the Elder. And if he will allow, talk, too, with the Wakuenai, Baniwa, Baré, Puinave, Warekena, and Tsase. Name the forest that I will show you."

He hears and quietly walks away into the forest. Then he sits and allows himself to be carried into the dream I provide.

The elder Krihisiwa is old with layers of wrinkled skin. He will soon return to the earth as we all must someday, yet he ventures out with Hekura and Daví while he still can, walking to the many nearby villages over many seasons as the earth moistens and dries and moistens again. And they rest in the village in between journeys. Along the way, the lovely Tanashina takes Daví by the hand to Hekura's section of the *shabono*. She had chosen him for a mate, taken by the smile he carries despite the heavy task he has been called upon to undertake. And they bring children into the world, children who will grow to eat the ashes of their father and of their mother while keeping the dream alive.

But long before that, the children, still little, sit to listen to the ceremonial *wayamou* that their father undertakes, and they hear his telling of the grandmother's spirit without naming me and telling of the task he has in life—their father and my son, Daví. So many ceremonies to the *wayamou*, a matter of persuasion to would-be enemies, followed by dancing and playing and feasting. For each group of visitors, the Tanashina-Daví clan builds a new *shabona*, thirty or forty long paces from beginning to end, formed in a circle, built with the hafted stone made into tools with which to chop wood. For each *wayamou*, there's a new temporary home of bamboo, wood, and palm; new tables for fruit, root and wood-burning pits for the hunt's well-cooked meat, maybe a peccary or a tapir; and then play, even a new romance here and there to help to bring would-be enemies together. All this will end as I had said, though not for many seasons to come. Daví will taste so little of the fruit of his labor, except, perhaps, when he is allowed to join me to look through the Record at the end of life-on-soil. In the meanwhile, there will be dancing with each success while he still lives.

For each *wayamou*, Daví dresses formally with large-feathered armbands and the smaller more colorful feathers through his earlobes.

The talking goes on for an entire night, replete with talk of sex when humor is called for or mild threats when necessary, and all of it given to repetition. This is the way of the *wayamou*: Daví says something, and the guest repeats with some modification, all delivered with broad gestures. Daví and his guest sit on their haunches, marking emphasis by broad swings of an arm and a slap back to the buttocks to make emphasis clear. And when it seems that the other is responsive, is ready to hear the reason for the meeting, Daví "names the forest," telling of the places known through dreams, the vision I had brought to Daví.

"As the toucan flies," Daví says while thrusting three long arrows clutched to his fist up above his head, "its feathers remain untouched. The land is black, and there is no bamboo."

"Ha!" says the other. "The toucan flies, its feathers untouched. There is no bamboo. The toucan alone survives, eh?" slapping his butt.

"The land *is* clear; the toucan *does* fly," says Daví. "And the land is black but bears fruit, and the manioc lies plentiful beneath the blackened soil. And there is sex all day and night, if she allows, with no need for the shelter of the bamboo and the feathers of the bird."

And it is understood that the toucan's tail feather is the fletching of an arrow, bamboo the arrow's shaft. There is peace, in other words. But the other has questioned at what cost—peace but nothing else. The other hears the blackened soil as barren soil, but Daví corrects it. He had seen in his vision that I provided this kind of creation, this farming, not barren land but what will be called *tala y roza*, a swidden. So fertile land and fertile people and less hunting and greater freedom from war.

Daví is calling for those who would rather not be warriors to venture to a place where farming can be created, where greater leisure will be possible. And the would-be opponent knows this place that Daví describes can only be the product of a dream, a dream inhabited by the spirit of one close to Daví. And even as the visitor knows who the spirit is, he will not name me, will not break the taboo and risk the peace they are negotiating. Daví's naming of the forest is credible.

Then, abruptly, the guest will say something like, "I will have one of your women who chooses me now." That marks the end of the *wayamou*, Daví making a final comment: "And we will have whoever of *your* women chooses us. And the women will boast of their power in being able to choose the leader of almost-an-enemy, boasting the wisdom of their selection, and they will whisper of their joy—and maybe we will know pleasure, too, if they allow. They will choose us as they desire."

Laughter. "Yes. That is good. Let us eat."

A successful *wayamou*.

During the feast the rhetoric changes, Daví and his guest speaking less metaphorically: a call to those who would seek a different kind of life, a conscious decision, not necessarily the migration that comes of fleeing an ongoing war or famine or a plague, but simply the possibility for peace in a fruitful and well-watered land, a rainforest that they can enter and from which they can depart, where fever is less frequent, where the people can grow strong and even discard the coverings of the body and live without shame.

III

Most of the people with whom Daví spoke remained in their villages. But there were many others, many from among them who joined Tanashina and Daví in their journey north, following the path that they laid out. No one group dominated among these seekers of peace so that no one tongue dominated. But the need to communicate, to find ways to cooperate in order not only to survive but in order to build, could not be denied. They had to talk with one another across their many tongues. So slowly, a pidgin, then a creole, and, eventually, a new tongue. And with the new tongue, new conventions, a tongue that the future will call Arawak and Lokono, and even later, Taíno. And the pilgrims are joined along the way by others, some driven by climate change, others running from slavery or serfdom under the hands of the empires of the north and the west, the Inca or Maya and later the Azteca, and yet others from lands far to the west and north of the travelers. And their tongues and even their cultures mixed. And they all became Arawak.

So I watched as Tanashina and Daví and the generations of their children passed away and into my world, so, too, Yarima with Krihisiwa the Elder, Roobemi and Hekura, and the children of the children. But the journey remained, those who had been warriors walking in front, negotiating the land and the land's obstacles, greeting new pilgrims or fending off those who feared the pilgrims were seeking to take the land of those who were already there. The arrow-bearers worked to keep the journey safe. And all, warrior or not, would tell stories of the past during quiet nights. And there were those whose major task was to be the storyteller. It was the storytellers who kept the people alive, who knew the family lines, who held the memory, who told of Tanashina and Daví, telling of me without naming me, and telling of the three mothers who guide me, stories that spread among the many. And since there were many or many different ways, most no longer ate the ashes of those who entered the spirit world but would spread the ashes on the water and the rivers, and they would sip the water so that many over time could see the memory of the storytellers. And some would stop to etch images of the stories on rock and tell of the gods.

The people of the River walked or navigated the rivers, and eventually the sea, on their *kanoa*; some *kanoa* holding many, as many as eighty, and some hollowed out to fit only one, form following function, all heading to the land I had promised, often stopping, sometimes for entire seasons, to fish, to hunt, even to grow food on mounds of dark rich soil that they had worked, the *conuco*. And some would say, "This is good. This is where we stay." And others would continue north, knowing that "good" was not the place prophesied.

And then there seemed nowhere else to go. They had come to the northernmost tip, facing the sea, water without end, and yet some would brave it.

IV

And these brave ones came upon an island that they named *Lëre*. And Lëre and the nearby island that they named *Tobanco*, named for the leaves they would burn and inhale, would also be good, even wonderous.

Yet among the Arawakans there remained a conservative group.

I will see this again and again during times of great change. Whenever change is threatening to be complete, changing customs and language and even the memory of things past, there rises a reactionary response. When these came up along the centuries of the journey, the conservative ones would splinter off to meet some other fate. Some would believe that the promise had not been met, that the soil was not what some believed was truly the promise fulfilled. So there arose the desire among some to hearken back to an imagined previous time, a time remembered as somehow greater than the present. It is always this way when change is deep.

Among the People whose stories I tell, there were the Kalina, unhappy with what they saw as a laziness among those who had settled in Lëre and Tobanco. As beautiful as the islands were, they could not believe these were the lands that had been promised. The rainforest was small and mountainous. This could not be Daví's land of promise. So, the Kalina ventured onward, believing there had to be more islands, and there were. But there were people already there, the Iñeri. The Kalina had been the warriors who had run point during the journey, still holding on to some older warrior ways. So, as warriors, the Kalina forcefully took and subsumed the Iñeri. And the Iñeri, in order to survive, became Kalina. But in so doing, the Kalina themselves changed. Together they became *Caribes*.

Others continued, following the islands north then west, and there they made their homes. And even as there were others already on one large island, the *Guanahatabeyes*, who lived along the western coast of the island they called *Colba*, the travelers who were not Kalina did not seek to conquer or to absorb but to live alongside. As far as the People were concerned, all were brothers and sisters, *Taíno*.

The Caribes had always been the warriors, even as others knew well the way with the spear or the arrow though more as tools for hunting or fishing— tools, not weapons, not as the means for establishing and maintaining power. And when the Caribes separated from the Taíno, the Caribes decided that the men alone would be the leaders, that the women would be slaves, reproductive property.

Eventually, the Strangers who will come from unknown places will see the Caribes as well-suited to being slaves because they were seen as strong, resilient, better suited to the labors of slavery than the too peaceful and thereby assumed weak Taíno. Caribes would be worthy of slavery because they captured and enslaved;

worthy of slavery because of the savagery of eating human flesh, the Caribes' reconstruction of the old ways, confusing the ashes as aids to memory with the eating of body parts in order to consume the desired qualities of the enemy, eating the arm of a particularly talented archer, for instance, or the brains of the cunning. The Strangers would even name the eating of the dead after them—*caribales*, the word changing as words do over time.

The others, Taíno, managed well in living with the others, the Guanahatabeyes who had traveled from the land that would long later be named *la Pascua Florida*, named after a flower festival in celebration of the Christian God's rising from the dead, a God so very much like Yúcahu. The Guanahatabeyes had willingly adopted many of the cultural ways of the Arawakans, those who possessed farming, art-on-rock, a shared history, and a shared belief in a loving afterlife.

The People, Taíno, had created a newer culture over time. The people who had traveled from the river they would come to call *Shingu* would be born anew in a cave, where the guard of the cave had fallen asleep and, having fallen asleep, had failed to mark the dawn so that the sun took the guard away, and how others who had left the cave to fish were turned into trees so that the treeless place, *la sabana*, would change; and a fruit, *el jobo*, the June plum, would be born of the trees. And those who continued to carry the tales of Tanashina and Daví would tell of *Yúcahu Vagua Maorocotí*, He of No Beginning and No End, whose mother Atabey is more powerful than he, as mothers always are to their children. And the Man is the first human creation; and some of the men tied *inriri* to their bodies— woodpeckers, so that their "branch" might be whittled. And they became Woman. Yet it would happen that there would be those for whom the branch would not belong or for whom the branch would remain despite being a woman, and the person would adjust, and the People would simply accept the adjustment. The Stranger, Invaders, will not understand the ease of transgender among the People, assuming that the Caribe had castrated the men in order to fatten a future meal. So foreign are the ways of the Taíno; so arrogant are the Invaders not to consider other possibilities.

For the People, man and woman are fundamentally the same so either can rule, though the men rule more often, both patriarchy and matriarchy, depending on who rose to *cacique*, administrative leader of the group, the one who presides more than decides, a presider, a president, some groups consisting of 3,000 people or more. And the custom became that men and women would only cut the hair above the eyes. And they refined the making of cloth from the bolls of the plant *sarobey*, the cotton used for cloth, and to make *hamacas* for sleeping, and looser webbed *hamacas* for capturing fish, and the women who had chosen a life-long mate would wear a cloth over their genitals as a signal to all of their decision, and the People would decorate themselves with white, black, or red paint over parts of their faces or even their entire body; and they would hang ornaments from their earlobes and wear *cibas*, stone beads tied to arms and necks; and the ruler, the *cacique* or *cacica*, would wear *guanines*, bronze crests plated in gold.

And the People would live on fish and birds and lizards and fruit and tubers. There were no mammals native to the land. And they would grow squash and peppers and, especially after yucca, *batata*, the sweet potato. They would cook such things over the fire pit they called *barbacoa*. And on religious occasions, they would inhale *tabaco* or *cogioba* with which to worship Atabey, Yúcahu, and other gods.

In this new land, the home was no longer the clan-shared *shabona* but the single-family home, *bohío*, with many houses creating a village, the *yucayeque*, marked by a town circle, the *batey*. Most of the *bohío* are round, made of wood and leaves and thatch. One of the *bohío*, however, would be rectangular, facing the *batey*. It was the *caney* rather than a *bohío*, marking the home of the *cacica* or *cacique*.

And the people of a *yucayeque* would gather in the *batey* to socialize or to play ball, the game pilgrims from the north had introduced long ago, though here the ball would be smaller and could bounce, made from the sap of the local trees. So they played *batos* in the circular *batey*, hitting the ball with a stick, then running around before the ball was caught and thrown with hand or hip or head to tag the runner trying to get back home. And in keeping with Taíno ways, the game would not be one of conquest but of journeys home. And when there would come the Center of Wind, the god

Jurakán prompted by the goddess Guabancex, the People would seek the caves, only to return home to rebuild and to continue.

Such were their lives as I watched.

I am Bushika. I am the story of the birth of a people and the changing of the People when another world enters and yet another.

2 Bushika Tells of Colón

prosonomasia [12]

I guess I'll never know if my elementary-school friend chose to be Charles Bermudez instead of Carlos. I know that Johnny Torres was really Juan. He chose to go by Johnny, just like Jarapolk Cigash wanted to be called Jerry. But Dad instructed me, let's say "firmly," not to accept Villain-new-ava, *to say that the double-l should be pronounced as a* y *(well, for one of the dialects of Spanish, and even for one dialect of Puerto Ricans) and the* e *is eh, not* ā.

And then there was a time not too long ago when the checkout clerks at the local supermarket were to show an older kind of respect: "Thank you, Mr. Jones," "Thank you, Ms. Smith" (sometimes met with "It's Mrs."). And I would patiently watch the checker figure out how to say my last name. I would be okay with Villain-new-ava, *a good effort. And if one would ask how I pronounce my name, I would say it the family way—vee-ya. And some would look and get it. And some would simply smile. Then there was the one who said, "That's an unusual name," to which I said (kindly), "Not for most of the hemisphere." A rose by any other name becomes something other than the rose that was.*

Bushika continues to tell of that other time.

Before the Invasion, time was realized but was not measured. What mattered was the soil, the sky's effects on the soil, the end of the life-of-flesh of an elder, or the return to the soil of the fevered. Even the gods resided on the soil, atop *el Yunque.* When the Invaders came, they brought a counting system, with each full passing of the seasons equaling a numbered year, *un año.* The Invaders' year one was marked by the birth of the Son of Myriam, but they called her *María.* The year of Contact was dated as AD 1492 (*Ante Christum natum,* after the birth of Christ, or *Anno Domini,* for short, the year of the Lord). Later, AD would become CE, the Common Era, common among the conquerors and the conquered of so much of the globe, an interesting rhetorical choice, a quiet assumption of global power, *common* rather than acknowledged as *invoked.* For the People of what would someday be the Indies of the West (never to be acknowledged by Colón, that these were not simply the then-known Indies of South Asia), the first Contact was more like Year Zero. The next year, 1493, would mark Year One, when the People came to understand that they could no longer claim their soil as their own.

II

Standing on the shore of the island Guanahani, three strange *kanoa* rise up from the line where sea meets sky. These *kanoa* are different, not made of hollowed trees but made of slats, like the walls of some *caneyes.* From within these strange *kanoa* rise branchless trees, as if growing from the belly of the boat. On each tree there hangs tightly woven *hamaca* to capture the wind and move the *kanoa.* This is interesting, this use of the wind, but less understandable are smaller cloths. They simply wave, these colored cloths with strange markings. The Taíno would not understand the very concept of a banner or that the images are of crowns atop the letters F and Y.[13]

The People along the shore watch as small *kanoa* appear from the belly of the larger one and are then lowered to the sea. Standing at the front of one of the small *kanoa* is a strange-looking man, taller than most of the People, skin the color of the inside of a guava, a nose like a slender beak of a parrot, white whisps of hair extending from cloth over the head. His whole body is covered in cloth. So strange, especially since other men on the *kanoa* seem to be wearing cloth only below the waist as they pull their strange looking *naje* to paddle forward. Some of the men have hair on their faces. The pale one and two of the hairy-faced fully clothed ones carry the cloth with the images tied to a spear as they approach the *cacique* Guacanagarix after coming aground.

Guacanagarix had been chosen from among the *caciques* of the five clans to meet the Strangers. The *cacica* Anacaona had led the quick discussion:

"How do we proceed? Do we resist? We see no bows on them, no arrows. Or are we already lost, the beginning of the end we were told would one day come?

"We cannot know the intention of these Strangers who have come from beyond what we have explored, islands we have not yet discovered, traveling in what look like large flat-bottomed *kanoa*, seeking we know not what, traveling without women, as far as we can see. We must hear them out. It is our way. So we, too, will meet them without our bows and spears. And you, Guacanagarix, so given to a gracious tongue, will speak for us."

This is how Colón will record the event:

> The only people I saw were young men, not one of them over thirty. They're very well built, with fine bodies and handsome faces. They have coarse hair, almost like a horse's tail, and wear it short. Their hair comes to just above their eyebrows, except for a few strands in back, which they wear long and never cut. They are the color of Canary Islanders— neither black nor white. Some paint themselves black, some white, some red, and others some other color. Some paint their faces, others the whole body, and others just their eyes or nose. They carry no arms and don't seem to know about them because I showed them swords and they took them by the edge and cut themselves out of ignorance. They have no iron. Their light spears are just canes without iron. Some of them have a fish tooth at the tip, and others have something else. They are fairly tall people, good looking and well built. I saw some with evidence of wounds on their bodies. When I made signs asking about this, they indicated that people came there from nearby islands to capture them and they defended themselves. I believed and still believe that these people who came to take them captive are from the mainland.[14]

Guacanagarix of the clan Marién stands before the Strangers, standing tall, his face calm—no smile but showing no fear. There are only three of these Strangers before him, and one, clearly the leader, looks sickly.

The sickly one with an excess of cloth pats his chest with his palm and says, "*Me llamo Cristóbal Colón.*" Guacanagarix, assuming that the Stranger is naming his people, makes the same gesture, then points to Colón and to himself, back and forth several times, and says "*Nitaíno.*"

Year Zero is a time of discovery for the Taíno and for the Christians. For the Strangers and the Taíno, what unfolds is a trade venture, each adding to the discovery of things not previously known: parrots, cotton, and maybe *hamacas* for sleep and a *hamaca* for capturing fish, in exchange for green-colored glass *cibas*, a red headcloth, or bells to hang from the ears. Colón could not help but be imperial and imperious, yet he was kind, even in his arrogance:

> Because they were very friendly to us, and because I could see they were a people who could likely be converted to our holy faith by love more than force, I gave some of them a few red caps and glass rosary beads, which they hung about their necks, and other cheap trinkets in which they took a great deal of pleasure and which made them marvelously friendly to us. When we had put off again, they came swimming up to our boats, bringing us parrots, balls of cotton thread, light spears, and many other things, which they traded with us for other things that we gave them, like little glass beads and hawk's bells. They took what we had and gave of their own very willingly. But they seem to be a very poverty-stricken people. All go about as naked as the day they were born.[15]

Despite taking a few of the Taíno with him to Castilla (so that they would learn to speak, even as his own Spanish was not great, and with no sense that it was he who should learn the Taíno tongue, since he was the guest), conquest of land seemed not to have been the goal, only trade and, of course, religious conversion.

Even long after the discovery turned into Invasion and Conquest, the Taíno and those from unseen islands would trade yams, yucca, cassava, beans, or maize in exchange for sugarcane from India and bananas from Guinea (which will later be called Ghana), coffee from Ethiopia, rice from Southeast Asia, oranges from China. And the naming of the places of these foods were often mistaken for the names of the foods. Boricuas still call bananas *guineos* and oranges are *chinas*. Trade: a sign of welcome.

In the Year Zero, Taíno and Stranger discover.

Alongside the one who the Taíno will soon know as "don Cristóbal" or "*señor*" or "*el Almirante*" is another overdressed man, darker, a nose more like the Taíno (ironically, or maybe typically, given the imperial mindset, called a "Roman nose," though Rome had nothing to do with the Taíno before Contact). The darker man has hairs above the top lip and running the length of the lip and hair like a line below the middle of his lower lip, not covering half the face like the others. He speaks to Guacanagarix, palm patting chest:

" '*Ana min Luis de Torres man Q'ishtala. Jina min baeid bahthan ean alKhan Alkabir.*"

Blank look. So he turns to Spanish:

"*Señor Nitaíno, me llamo Luis de Torres. Venimos de lejo buscando el Gran Can.*"

And again Guacanagarix smiles and nods.

Colón says, "These kind people have no idea what you're saying, don Luis."

Don Luis is the Jewish translator the Admiral brought along to translate to Arabic, which was assumed to be the lingua franca of the Orient. But since the translator has not been understood, don Cristóbal concludes that the man and the people of this place must be of the islands off India, and since neither the Admiral nor don Luis knew Awadhi or classical Sanskrit, gestures would have to do. Besides, if they are in India, Colón had nevertheless succeeded in traveling west to arrive east, as far as he was concerned. Language, for Colón, is but a minor setback in an otherwise successful mission.

The Admiral never failed to believe that he had successfully traveled to the East by traveling west on the Ocean Sea. He knew, as was assumed by all, all of Colón's world and all of Taíno, that the world is a ball.[16] And though all from Colón's world assumed that there would be other lands on the ball, no other lands had yet been mapped. So, since the lands off India had not appeared on Colón's charts or maps, he named them and christened them, not caring that the People already had names for their lands and that, as far as the People were concerned, their land was already blessed.

Seeing the people naked and bearing no signs of the glories and wonders of the East—no fine robes of silk, no fine wine, no porcelain crockery, no gunpowder, not even the bejeweled loincloths of the Indians that had been described by one of the people of Colón's world—Marco Polo—Colón assumed that these were abandoned and neglected Indians, outcasts. For all that, he writes to his *cacica* and *cacique* that:

> They are so affectionate and have so little greed and are in all ways so amenable that I assure your Highnesses that there is in my opinion no better people and no better land in the world. They love their neighbours as themselves and their way of speaking is the sweetest in the world, gentle and smiling.[17]

When he left some of his crew behind, since the Santa María had run aground, Colón knew that his men would be treated well by the people of Guacanagarix and that his men would return the good treatment in kind (though they didn't), promising Guacanagarix in the bits of language that developed between the People and the Strangers, that when he returned, he would help the People tame their enemy, the Caribes, the monstrous man-eaters (which he didn't believe really existed, so an easy promise to make).

Year One would mark the beginning of the colony that has not yet ceased to be a colony.

The Goddess of the Wind, Guabancex, sought to delay the Admiral's return to his Castilla, pushing his ships to the place called Portugal. In the village Lisbon, where Colón had once lived and where his brother Bartolomeo had long lived, Colón sought an audience with the cacique, the king, João Segundo. The king and his council quickly realized that the People brought by the Admiral were not of the Orient, that don Cristóbal had nothing to say of houses of marble and gold, nothing of the bustling of trade on the ports, nothing of men and women dressed in silk, no talk from Colón, his men, nor the captured Taíno of the Great Khan; in short, nothing of Marco Polo's descriptions of the Orient. The conclusion, then, was that Colón had discovered new lands.

And so it began.

King João Segundo petitions the pope, saying that there is already an agreement in place that would surely suggest that whatever Colón had found would belong to Portugal. King João asks the Pope, Alejandro Sexto, to confirm João's understanding. But this pope had not always been "Alejandro." He was first known as Rodrigo Lanzol y de Borja of the House of Borgia (the family name adopted with the move from Spain to Italy). Before Alejandro/ Rodrigo was named pope, he had been a noble of Aragón, the area ruled by Fernando. The Pope was not about to side with King João.

In the time in between Years Zero and One, Alejandro Sexto issues a papal bull, a public announcement, the Inter caetera, giving Aragón, Castilla, and Portugal (to a lesser degree) the right to convert and the right to colonize and the right to enslave, enslaving both the new people of the Indies and the purchased people of Africa.

This is the beginning. A new kind of journey.

Armed with the blessing of the one the Christians called their Holy Father, Colón returns to the Islands, not with three ships but with seventeen. Twelve hundred men. Some will become rulers of the islands and of the People: the first Spanish ruler of Cuba, Diego Velázquez de Cuéllar; the first governor of Jamaica, Francisco de Garay; and the first governor of Boríkén, Juan Ponce de León. Among those less concerned with conquest and plunder is Pedro de las Casas, the father to the good Fray Bartolomé. And with the men come dogs and horses and sugar cane with which to make rum. Whatever Colón might have thought of the People, he had been overruled by aristocrats, a king, a queen, and the mortal Christian father of them all, the Pope.

Once they arrive, Doctor don Diego Álvarez Chanca writes of a couple of events:

> On Thursday, the 14th of November, the Admiral stopped at another island which he called Sancta Cruz; and he sent men ashore to capture some natives, and thus learn their

language. They seized four women and two children, and, as they were returning in the rowboat, they encountered a canoe, which contained four Indians and an Indian woman; when the Indians realized that they could not flee, they, including the woman, began to defend themselves; they began to fire arrows, and they wounded two Christians, and the woman even pierced a shield with her arrow; the sailors crashed their boat into the canoe and overturned it; one of the Indians, who had not lost his bow, swam and fired his arrows with almost the same vigor as if he had been ashore. They saw that one of the Indians had his generative instrument cut off; the Christians believed it was so the he could grow fatter, like a capon, then the Caribs would eat him. . . [F]rom there, he reached another large island, which he called Sanct Juan Baptista, which we now call Sanct Juan, and which, as we mentioned before, was called Boriquén by the Indians, in a bay of the island toward the west, where all the ships caught many kinds of fish. . . . Several Christians went ashore and walked to some houses that were very artfully made, although all were of straw and wood; and there was a plaza, with a road reaching from it to the sea, very clean and straight, made like a street; and the walls were of crossed or woven cane; and above, beautiful gardens, as if they were vineyards or orchards of orange or citron trees, such as there are in Valencia or in Barcelona; and next to the sea there was a high watchtower, where ten or twelve people could fit, also well made; it was probably the pleasure house of the lord of that island.[18]

If ever a language of the colonizer, then surely this. A watchtower to watch for the coming of the winds brought by the god Jurakán becomes a place for secret sex, since *el doctor* don Diego sees nothing worthy of a watchtower in his limited knowledge of where he is. And to him, it is remarkable that a woman would be a warrior. And the warrior who knew "himself" to be a woman is rendered a castrated rooster for a Carib meal. The truth is beyond the limited imaginations of the Invaders, imaginations that need not be taxed, since the imperial way was, no doubt, the right way, according to the imperial observers.

And even when their imagination was kind, it was often wrong—and not reconsidered. Don Colón and the others had decided that *Taíno* meant "good" or "noble," spoken repeatedly as the Invaders approached.

But *Taíno* is not just the naming of a particular people; it is *all* people, the Guanahatabeyes, the warring Caribes, and even the Invaders. The good and noble People were indeed making a plea to the Invaders: "*Taíno, Taíno, Taíno*"—hands extended to point to the Invaders then drawn to the chest, "You, me; we are kin," said again and again. We are all related, all kin. The sisterhood and brotherhood of humanity, such a Christian idea, not even guessed at by the Christians.[19]

This was the beginning, when kindness no longer mattered, except to be seen as weakness, when, apart from the occasional conflict with Caribes-as-invaders, the Taíno, the name that lasts, did enjoy the promised peace. And as promised, the peace lasted 1500 years. But the peace has passed, and all is justified by creating a sorting of value, *raíces* to *razas*, from roots to races. *Race*, the bane that remains, even as the idea that value is in the blood is no longer truly accepted ("truly" because "*la sangre llama*," "the blood beckons," is still a common expression for knowing one's "own kind.")

3 Yuíza

synecdoche, irony [20]

*Dad's discharge papers at the end of World War II read "WPR"
under "Race": White Puerto Rican. Mom would also have been a WPR,
though that never appeared on any official forms that I know of. Mom
was very proud of what she saw as my white features, saying that I had
"good hair" and "una nariz fina," what would commonly be called a
Roman nose, "pero eso' labios" ah, but those lips! Full lips, let's say.
For all that, when my sister was born, dark and curly haired, Dad would
call her his "trigueñita," his little dark one. In the neighborhood I
was "blanquito," which I took (as someone not living in Puerto Rico)
as "little whitey" rather than little-privileged-one, more the intent, I
eventually learned. Blanquito, is the term I got as one whose nariz fina
was always in a book. Over time, and away from Brooklyn, I was taken
for Italian or Jewish or Persian or South Asian, something ethnic, that
racialized ambiguous word, ethnic. Racism is always apparent, even
when race is ambiguous or declared a fiction. The wonder of believing to
know so much about a person or a people based on so little.*

Yuíza was *cacica* of the village Jaymanio in the area known as
Yu-ke, el Yunque, the rainforest. She was born the year after Colón
arrived on Borikén, 1494. Hers was an unusual beauty: the light
cinnamon-brown skin of the Taíno, cat's eyes with irises more
black than brown. And there was something in the light that shone
from those eyes, something different, somehow different from her
siblings. There was simply something else about her. Her parents
knew it. Her sisters and brothers knew it. The villagers knew it.

Yuíza was fourteen-years-old, sitting with her mother and others in front of the family *bohío*, laughing over something said when I appeared visible to all, dressed as I would have when I was of the flesh, wearing the red loincloth made of palm-leaf fiber, not the cotton of the Taíno. I still wore my piercings, and my hair appeared in the custom of the Yanomami.

I looked directly at Yuíza and said in the language of the Christians, "*las tres razas.*" Nothing more.

On that day in the Christian year 1508, the People of Jaymanio anointed Yuíza their *cacica.* And she ruled for seven years, up to the day of her execution.

II

He was a young man of nobility from Santervás de Campos in Valladolid, León, under the rule of Ysabel and Fernando. To say that he was "slender" would suggest that there was more meat to his frame than there was. His beard, too, was slight: whisps of hair along his jaw, hair neither truly red nor truly brown. And from his chin, he wore longer whiskers, coming to two points like the serpent's tongue.

He was but eighteen, a volunteer during the last year of Castilla's and Aragón's war against the Emirate of Granada. The Catholic Monarchs had completed the reconquest of the peninsula, the end of al-Andalus. And in the process, the young man of León discovered an appetite for risk and for conquest. He longed for more. The Admiral don Cristóbal, visiting the Monarchs at Santa Fe where the last battle had been won, had just requested to partake a second voyage. So, as a noble and a former volunteer in the service of their Majesties, Juan Ponce de León sought and was granted permission to join don Cristóbal's expedition.

The journey takes him to the island of Ayiti, renamed *Española* by Colón. The sun is warm, the water like blue-filtered glass, the beaches white sand. And the trees contain guava; *guanabana*; cherimoya, the fruit the monks called "the Flower of the Five Wounds;" the fruit that comes of the Flower of the Passion of Christ, passion fruit. Ponce seeks an audience with the Royal

Governor and Supreme Judge of the Indies, Fray Nicolás de Ovando y Cáceres to see if there might be a way he could remain in Española permanently.

"Well, young fellow, I don't see a current need for a military man. These *Indios* are too lazy to cause any trouble. And they are protected by the Queen, who has commanded that the Indians are to be regarded as vassals of Castilla, to be no less under royal protection than any other loyal subject, even though they are not our equals. Then again, you do have the ear of Our Most Holy Lady and Lord, so, yes, you can remain as a lieutenant."

Fray Nicolás was loyal but no less clever. If the Indians could not be slaves, they could be servants. And since the *negros* and *mulatos* are not Indians, and thereby not vassals, they could indeed be used as slaves.

The queen also decided that the *encomienda* system that had been applied to the conquered Moors in her homeland should also be used in the colonies. On the one hand, the system was a way of seeking tribute from the conquered through labor. On the other, it was a trust in which the conquered would receive military protection and other benefits. Fray Nicolás, ever obedient, awarded parcels of land to *conquistadores* and nobles, provided they understood that the land still belonged to the conquered, the Indians. A *cacique* would appoint the servants to work the land with the *encomendero*, the overseer of the trust. And in keeping with the workings of a trust, which implies an exchange between trustor and trustee, the People would receive lessons in the Spanish language and the means with which to convert to Christianity: land and labor in exchange for spiritual salvation. The Taíno would remain servants by title, but they would be slaves by treatment.

And when there was resistance to slave-like labor, resistance was met with cruelty. Lashes of the whip. Stampeded by an *encomendero* on horseback. Sliced by a Toledo-steel sword. Crucified and fed to dogs. Left to starve. Or simply shot. So some Taíno ran inland; some paddled their way to other islands; some committed suicide. And some gathered in rebellion, a matter Fray Nicolás never imagined, having mistaken kindness for weakness.

In the city of Higüey, on the far east of the Island Española, the *cacique* Cotubanamá organized a revolt. The governor, Fray Nicolás, sent Lieutenant Juan de Esquivel to quash the rebellion, with Lieutenant Ponce as Esquivel's Number Two. The rebellion is easily crushed.

But the People are resilient.

So there comes a second rebellion. This time, Lieutenant Ponce is in charge. And with him are armed *negros auxiliares*, comprised of Black and mulatto freemen, and *libertos* along with Black and mulatto slaves who hope to win their freedom by fighting alongside the Spaniards. *Los negros* serve as infantry while the nobles attack on horseback with attack dogs, the nobles wielding swords, slaughtering warriors, women, children, the elderly, anyone and everyone. The good Brother Bartolomé writes to the monarchs in protest. He writes that Ponce de León's actions are excessive, but the monarchs only recognize courage and profit, so they reward don Juan. Soon after he finds and kills Cotubanamá, Ponce de León is appointed regional governor of Higüey. The new governor then enslaves the survivors of the revolt, forcing them to cultivate his land and work the mines. No more pretense that this was the Indians' land. Juan Ponce de León becomes wealthy, selling food and supplies to those who would journey from Higüey back to Ibérica. And he, too, visits the peninsula, where he meets and marries Leonora.

Yet the adventurer don Juan still thirsts for adventure. So—to Borikén with King Fernando's blessing. Ponce de León, with fifty men and a number of horses, travels to Borikén and establishes the city of Caparra, west of what will become San Juan.

There, in the Christian year 1508, he meets with Borikén's most honored *cacique*, Agüeybaná.

"*Soy el Marqués* Juan Ponce de León," hand patting his heart.

"*Y yo soy el gran cacique* Agüeybaná."

The exchange is in accordance with Taíno ways in which initial exchanges, called *guaytiao*, assume peace and friendship. Agüeybaná's mother had told him that the choice upon meeting the Christians would be between slaughter and compliance. He complied.

Ponce de León has a fine home built on Caparra where he is joined by his family a year later in 1509.

1510: Agüeybaná falls victim to one of the new diseases carried by the Christians. The germs they carry are greater killers of the Taíno than all the soldiers and weapons of Europe. Agüeybaná's brother, Güeybaná, assumes the role of primary leader. He will be forever remembered as *Güeybaná el Bravo*.

And in that same year, 1510, King Fernando grants Ponce de León the titles of "Captain of Land and Sea" and "First Justice of the Island of San Juan."

Now, what made Güeybaná courageous, *el Bravo*, was his orchestration of the rebellion of 1511, the "Spanish and Taíno War of San Juan, Borikén." Güeybaná and a number of regional *caciques* organize the Island's Taíno to launch direct attacks against the Christians. But Ponce de León and his *conquistadores* have superior weaponry. The attacks fail.

The People adjust, resorting to little wars, *guerillas*, even after *el Bravo* is killed. Soldiers are dispersed among the People, with the *libertos* of the Black Auxiliary assigned to less strategic sites, like the mountains, away from the ports.

Juan Ponce de Léon leaves Borikén that year.

And in his absence the local friars complain that the environment of Caparra is not good for newborns. They want to move the capital to the islet and port, *el Puerto Rico*. The islet reminds the friars of their home on the Gran Canary. They get their way. This will become the city of San Juan.

III

In the mountains, Yuíza sits among the elders to try to explain what she knows of *las tres razas* and to try to explain her decision to marry the dark tall *liberto* who sports a full curly beard with skin no different in color than hers or any of the Taíno, his hair often worn in a braid, hair the color of bronze, *guanín*, not quite red, not quite the color of gold; his nose no different from the Taíno; and eyes the color of leaves in the sunlight. Pedro Mejías, Pepe, is one the Christians call *un mulato*, a mule-like one, what comes of breeding a thoroughbred with a donkey, a mule, say the Invaders.

Yuíza speaks:

"The goddess who appeared before us seven years ago was not Atabey."

From the circle:

"Yes, yes. We could see that," spoken by Aguayex, the elder of the council, maybe even sixty-years-old, maybe older. He speaks in the emerging creole of Taíno, a mix of the Spanish of the Andalusian and the Spanish of the Guanche.

Aguayex: "Not Atabey, but surely a Shingu goddess, no?"

"Don't know. But I do know she was sent by the three virgin mothers, Atabey, Candelaria, and María. Of that, I am sure, even as I don't know what that means, don't know why our mother, and the mother of the Guanche, and the Christian mother would send us a messenger. Or what that message means. I only know what I have learned from my travels to Ayiti where I have spoken to *la Lengua*, don Cristóbal Rodríguez, he who can speak in many tongues. And I have learned from my Pepe, he who most serves me, who is my heaven."

"Ay, Yuíza, we know what the mule serves," from Aguayex. Loud laughter from the council. But Yuíza is serious, not of a mind for wordplay.

"Please, put all that aside for now and just hear me! Pepe is not the same as these lovers of power above all else. When they are done with us, they will try to wipe us from this land, from *our* land. You all know that! You know how close we have come to joining our ancestors—all of us—almost wiped from memory. That we are here speaking in council is only because of where we are, above the rest and under the cover of our wide leaves and the rain. And maybe we would not even be here if not for the Caribes who joined in the fight. And we surely would not be here but for *la encomienda*."

Heads tilt, brows furrow, mouths curve downward, gestures of incredulity, even absurdity.

"No! I mean it! The slaughter would have been complete if they had not needed our bodies to labor for their silver and gold. The numbers of *los negros* and those they call *mulatos* are still too few to replace us for the labor they need done but will not do themselves.

"I speak to you of survival with the greatest of respect, my elders. And I say—I believe—that those like Pepe Mejías are a means to our survival. You joke about my mule. And, yes, of course my body desires. How not? But so does my mind. And so does my soul, aching for freedom. And I believe my thinking is tied to *raza*, to the words spoken by the Spirit."

And so she speaks as best she can of what she learned from the men of Spain. *La Lengua* had told her of Spain and Portugal and of mountains that led to all of Europe. As far as she could figure, this "Europe" was like the lands of the Muskogee, the Yuckis, the Yamasses, and all the peoples north, and the Timucuan, the Tequesta, the Chahta, the Diné, the Tenochca, and the Azteca, the Maya, and the Shingu.

"This Europe," she says, "must be like the vastness of our trade routes and all the lands and the people beyond. It is the whole of their many peoples and their towns larger than Caparra. Theirs is a land named after something of a goddess."

Blank looks.

"Look; I am told that there is a large body of land that is Christian, and it is called Europe, after a princess or goddess, Europa. It seems that this Europe is like our Abya Yala, the mature land."

Yuíza had yet to speak directly of *raza*. But that is the People's way—a full round way, a wandering that is not truly a wandering, a telling that is a teaching along the way. Not a tangent but a full context. And the context for *raza* is conquest.

"Within this Europe is the land of Spain and Portugal. But the land of these Christians is isolated, what they call *una península*, an incomplete island, like the land of the Timucua speakers that don Juan calls *la Florida*.

"The greatest rulers of Europe according to *la Lengua* and to Pepe were in Roma, a city in a land they call *Latium*. And they say that there was a Roman storyteller who told of a hero of the peninsula, or maybe even a god, named Hispan or Espan, so that these Romans named the land of the peninsula for him, a leader or a god of the time when the people who spoke the tongue *Celta Galo* ruled the peninsula. So when Roma took the peninsula and the land above the mountains and the land below the peninsula's sea, where Mejías' people come from, they kept the name España."[21]

Yuíza stops to look in the eyes of the elders. They are listening but not understanding, their brows not only furrowed and eyes narrowed but turned inside, trying to picture what they are hearing. Some chuckle or sneer. Such nonsense. Yet the elders are lovers of tales. So they listen to Yuíza while they smoke tobacco, since to talk of spirits must mean this is a religious event, no?

She says that the peninsula had been ruled by these Celt speakers from deeper within Europe's lands and then the Romans and then others, Goths, and then yet others, Moors. And there were Jews, who weren't conquerors but travelers, forced to travel after the Romans had taken these Jews' land. But the Jews are great survivors, and sometimes they did gain a kind of power. Yet each time they did they would be crushed again, only to rise again. And there are the people of Africa, the black ones who began to live among the Christians and the Taíno. And there are those like Mejías with skin colored like the Taíno but with hair of orange-yellow. The Spaniards, like the Romans before them, assumed that these Guanches must have once been black, but the Guanches believe they are remnants of a lost continent called Atlantis. Still, for the Spaniards, Africa is black and Europe is not, even as they know of India and Cathay and Japan, of people neither black nor white. For all that, skin color is not *raza*, not yet, not really. The Guanches are from islands off Africa, so they must have once been black, the Spaniards decided. And if from Africa, they must be less than the superior Christians, *mulatos.*

"But my tall bronze-haired mate is no mule," spoken with a smile. And the elders laugh, raising their eyebrows.

"Good. Humor," Yuíza thinks.

But Yuíza had been retelling without truly knowing. Her mind's eye could only see what it had seen, her ear what it had heard. She had seen the *conquistadores*, could see their commonalities, yet her ear heard that some spoke a Spanish that was not the tongue of their mothers, that their tongue betrayed other language roots. *La Lengua's* stories told of many people of this Europe and of a place from which many tongues formed, a place called Babel. And maybe those were the roots, *las razas*, the word for slivers of a root, derived, likely, from *raíces*.

She had been spouting words. And as all leaders must be persuaders, she carried herself well. And the elders had indeed been listening, trying to understand and to believe. But in her heart Yuíza knew that she did not know, that she was simply spouting the words of *la Lengua* and Pepe. If she were going to explain the significance of "*las tres razas*," she would need to understand better, more fully, so she decides that when the laughing was done, she would call for food and drink, the sign that the meeting would be in recess, call it a day and not betray her own confusion.

That evening as she sits alone on her favorite *duho*, the beautifully carved chair with the high back, she decides she would snuff *cohoba* out of the long pipe, maybe to dream and maybe to walk and to talk among the spirits. She knows that in the morning she would have to say more of *raza*. She prays for guidance.

And as she sits and as she prays, she watches the sun set, knowing that the nausea from the *cohoba* would soon pass as she entered the world of spirits. And pass it does. Then the shivers come, like hairs standing on end but under the skin, and then the swelling inside her head, the oily tears, the bright sparkling colors, watching the waves of heat shimmering from the ground as dusk turns to dark and the coqui frogs start their calming mating calls, "co-kee, co-kee." And if she does nothing but sleep, she says to herself, she would at least wake up refreshed, maybe better prepared to meet the elders yet again and convey what she had learned more fully.

IV

And as Yuíza slipped into dream, I entered her dreams, helping her to recall and to imagine the conversations concerning the Christians, recall and imagine this matter of *raza*.

The history of *raza* is the history of conquest, changed radically with the conquest that crossed the Ocean.

And with conquest, the ways of the conqueror seep into the minds of the conquered, layers over the memory of what the conquered once were before the conquest, hardening like cooled lava, the rock that melts then covers the earth while the first earth lies beneath, forgotten, so that the conquered begin to inflict that which had been inflicted and believe it is as it always was. One must look to when the lava flowed. Then, perhaps, the memory of the time before the conquests conquered minds can be remembered. To know of the people of what Amerigo Vespucci will call "a new world"[22] is to know of the world, a world that developed racism from races, slivers of roots, like "a race of ginger." Roots to races becomes a means with which to justify the new exploitation that became possible with Europe's stumbling onto the world that was new to Europe, creating what would come to be called "the modern world order."[23] I will have to show Yuíza.

Yuíza's dreams try to envision Rome in the way *la Lengua* had described it, but his telling of Rome's slaves is of people from all of Rome's known world, more than Africans, more than she can visualize without my help. And so I whisper of a storyteller, Virgilio, and I draw pictures with words, Virgilio's story of a boy who would save and rule the world.[24] And I bring Yuíza to the sounds of other storytellers who say that Virgilio's story was of the son of María, Jesús, who was born a Jew. And if this boy was the Christian son of God, then those not Christian or Jew would be *ethnica*, non-believers. And if non-believers, then surely inferior to the believers. This was not yet the birth of *raza*, yet this word—*ethnic*— would remain folded into race, or so I whisper into the soul of the *cacica*.

The true birth of *raza*, begins, I say, with the invasion of the Berber Tariq ibn-Ziyad, with the words that *la Lengua* had read to her, explaining that as soon as these Moors had landed on Spain, the leader Tariq had all their ships burned. And he said to his warriors the words I whispered in the sounds of a man's voice:

> "Oh, my warriors, so now where will you go? Behind you is the sea; before you is the enemy. All you have left now is your courage and your faith. Remember that in this land you

are more unfortunate than the orphan seated at the table of the selfish master. Your enemy approaches, protected by an immense army. He has so many men. You have your scimitar. It, your courage, and your faith are your only chance for life, the life you can snatch from the hands of your enemy.

"Forget the disgrace of flight of which you dream and instead attack this monarch who has left his strongly fortified city to meet you. Here is a splendid opportunity to defeat him, if you will consent to expose yourselves freely to death.

"And I do not just tell you to do what I do not. I will face the dangers with you. I will ride before you, be the first to tempt death. Remember that if you suffer some, you will be rewarded with supreme delight. Do not imagine that your fate can be separated from mine. If you fall, I will either fall with you or avenge you.

"You have heard that in this country there are a great number of ravishingly beautiful maidens from the land of the Hellenes. They walk in their graceful forms, draped in sumptuous gowns on which gleam pearls, coral, and the purest gold. The Commander of True Believers, al-Walid son of Abd al-Malik, has chosen you for this attack from among all his Arab warriors. As such he promises that you shall become his comrades and shall hold the rank of kings in this land. Such is his confidence in your brave spirits. The one fruit which he desires to obtain from your bravery is that the word of Allah shall be exalted throughout this land, and that the True Religion shall be established here, while the spoils will belong to yourselves.

"Remember as we move forward, that I place myself in the front of this glorious charge which I exhort you to make. At the moment when the two armies meet face-to-face, smelling each other's breaths, you will see me, never doubt it, seeking out this Roderick, this tyrant of his people, challenging him to combat, praise Allah Most Great."[25]

Yuíza, even in her dream, remembers that *la Lengua* said that Tariq might well have read the story of yet another storyteller from the first conquerors of the peninsula, a blind man, Homero, who had placed a very similar speech in the mouth of a soldier with which to speak to his leader: honor, duty, fame, wealth, women, the will of the gods.[26] He might be right. I am the memory of the People and those who conquered, but the Record does not go to those ancient times, at least not yet.

Yet, whether Homero or Tariq or Fernando and Ysabel, these are the terms of conquest to convince those who have little to gain in conquest to take part: the occupation of fertile land, conversion, and the promise of titles and riches. And I make sure that Yuíza knows this, in her mind, in her soul.

Tariq's conquest begins the Arab Moors' 800-years of rule in the peninsula, and rebellion after rebellion ensues, just as the Boricuas rebel against the Christians. Eight hundred years will pass before al-Andalus will give the final ground, reduced to Andalucía, the name that remains, even after King Fernando and Queen Ysabel sponsor the ventures of the Admiral don Cristóbal and the Taíno become subject to what the Spaniards themselves had endured.

"In the process of reconquering the peninsula, *la Reconquista*, there begins the history of *razas*, races," I whisper.

The Christians and the Muslims and the Jews each believe that they alone are believers of the True Faith, even as they each believe in the same God and as they each believe they are descended from the same earthly father, Abram.

They are three with essentially the same beliefs even if in different tongues and with different rituals, differences in ways being confused with differences in nature. *Raza* might have begun as a word for lineage and ancestry, the people being descended from a common source, each person a sliver from the roots of a family's or people's tree. Jews, Christians, and Muslims all claimed the same roots, Abram and the God of all gods, with a different name for each faith, yet all believing in Moses as messenger. The Christian God, who is God of the Torah, who is God of the Quran is like Atabey but is Father, not Mother, of all including the father of His mother, Miryam, María, who is not a goddess even as she is honored among Jews, Muslims, and Christians, though to different degrees.

Yet even as they make the same claim as to bloodline and roots, they base *race* on differences in roots, different lineages, different bloodlines.

Race is based on difference when we all are the same. "This is *irony*," I whisper.

The races are enemies, different, but different *because* they are the same while they compete for whatever it is they desire. The conqueror *needs* the conquered to be different.[27] This is the true irony of all racism. All are the same being.

This is the irony of Christians marking roots different from Muslims and Jews. They are kin, of one ancestry according to their beliefs, but they are enemies in the need for power, power over people, power over the land of the people, the things they value in the land that is otherwise rare, like gold or even nutmeg or black pepper, and all of this creation of differences that are mainly superficial becomes spoken in convincing otherwise good people that those being conquered are somehow inferior. Good people would be less likely to enslave equals. The people *must* be different, even down to the very blood that runs through them.

But race does not end with the irony of Muslim, Christian, and Jew, though it begins there.

And Yuíza remembers *la Lengua's* description of the man he calls *pope*, carrying a *ferula, una caña*, a stick with a cross on top. She knows of the cross, of course, and its story. And in her dream, she remembers telling *la Lengua* that she did love the stories of this man of peace, the son of María, but she could not understand the evil done in His name. Another irony, the thinking aloud that dreams contain, dreaming of the thought of the self of the dream.

La Lengua had described a man in raggedy robes, Francis, who spoke to the Pope about the need for the Pope to be humble, just like Jesús was humble. And the Pope smiles, she "sees" in her dream, and she hears him say he agrees with Francis. And I insert the sounds so that she hears the words:

"It is just, Brother Francis, to remind me that just as Jesús was a humble man of physical labor, not only a son of Abraham but of the root of David, Jesús, the son of God who preferred to claim being a son of man, I, too, must be humble, since I cannot rise to the glory of Our Lord.

"Yet, my Brother, how am I to allow the Muslims' belief that María was the Virgin Mother of the Chosen One yet in the same breath deny the crucifixion? Or what do I do with the Jews, who do not see Jesús as a son of David at all, never mind God, but as a son of Joseph, denying the Immaculate Conception? It is no wonder that Jews are doomed to wander, bearing the mark of Cain. Yet here they are, walking alongside the people of Aragón and Castilla, treated like natives to the lands, free to deliver homilies drawn from Hebrew misreadings of the Holy Word? Do I shun my responsibility in allowing such heresy? Yes, Francis, I must, as you say, remain humble. But I cannot allow such Muslim and Jewish arrogance."

And Yuíza understood yet another irony: the arrogant one calling others arrogant, even if *la Lengua's* telling and the voices I inserted are not true word-for-word but true in the sentiment of what had happened.

Then I tell of this "humble" and "innocent" father of fathers, this pope, sending a nobleman to slaughter all the people of Gaul, Jews and Christians alike, declaring that God will do the necessary sorting at the gates of Heaven. And Yuíza remembers being told that Fernando and Ysabel did insist that Jews and Muslims were either to convert to Christianity or leave the land. And many did convert, just as she herself had done so that she and her Pepe could be together. But conversion does not stop the distrust, that these *conversos* were saying whatever was necessary to survive, but in truth they could not change their nature. That was the contradiction to compliance that the ones in power chose to believe, that Jewish blood would continue to course through their veins.

This does not bode well for her and Mejías, Yuíza realizes even in her dreams, even as she feels the coming of a child from the love between her and her Pepe, just as she had joked with the elders that Pepe is no sterile mule.

And she realized that I could not have meant that *las tres razas* simply meant Christian, Muslim, and Jew. Yuíza knew that I had to mean the People, the ones the Invaders called "Indians," as well as the Africans and the Christians. This new child, her heart said in her dream, would be the key to Taíno survival—the creation of a new race.

V

Yuíza smells the morning dew and feels the heat of sunlight on her lids, and on her lap is a heavy weight. Yuíza rubs off the crustiness around her eyes, opening them to the dawn, stretching to realize that she is still seated on her *duho*. Looking down, she sees her Pepe's head on her lap, his body stretched on the skin of a yagua palm as he still sleeps, dressed only in the breeches of his uniform. On seeing him, she feels the swelling of love within that place within the chest that cannot be measured as she thinks of the child to come of this romance. But she also knows deep in her heart that the People will not win in its wars against the Invaders, even as they become Boricuas, no longer fully Taíno. Awakening Mejías, she says they have much to discuss, but first she must speak with the elders.

"I have known a journey, and I have spoken with the Spirit. I'll be brief. The three races are the Africans, the Christians, and us, the People, and our survival will depend on accepting that the forest—all of the land—will need to be shared. That is as it is—*eso e' lo que es*. So let us now celebrate these days that remain while the forest is still mostly ours."

This is her hope, but not truly her belief.

Yuíza fully adopts her Christian name, Loíza, and becomes large with child—*Taíno, mestizo, mulato—pardo*, more than *mestizo*, the three races as one: *pardo*. A boy. And they name him Abora, a name that has a Spanish sound to it but is the name of the supreme god of the Guanche from La Palma, the Canary Islands.

The governor in that year, 1512, is Cristóbal Mendoza. He is a military man, harsh and vicious in his treatment of the Taíno. But when cruelty grows harshest, compliance is the last thing to come of it. What comes is rebellion. So rebels destroy the city of San Germán, then the rebels paddle to the bay of Puerto Rico and set fire to Caparra. And in their bloodlust, they decide to kill Yuíza-the-Race-Traitor, her *mulato* man, and their *pardo* child. But Mejiás and

Abora had ventured into the forest on a simple exploration. While they are away, Yuíza is caught and lynched from a tree. Dead.

Mejías, now fearing for the life of their child, gathers Abora and heads down the mountain and north to a quiet land along the ocean coast. He names the land after his love—Loíza Aldea, the Village of Loíza.

Over time, Loíza Aldea becomes a safe haven for runaway African slaves, and under the wise leadership of the *cacique* Abora the people are encouraged to create a Boricua culture that contains *las tres razas*—Taíno, Guanche-African, and Christian. Every year, they celebrate the feast of the patron saint of Spain, the Apostle James, with *la Festival de Santiago Apóstol*, the festival including *vejigante* masks of the Taíno tradition and the African dances that eventually become the traditional music and dance of Puerto Rico, *bomba y plena*, all within the Christian title and rituals.

4 From Alicia the Corsair
concessio [28]

Mama Pina, my father's mother, mi abuelita, was a spiritualist. When someone died in the neighborhood, the corpse was brought to Dad's home, placed on the dinner table, the table brought into the living room. And Mama Pina would bring assurances (or telling silences). As she spoke with the other world, Dad as a boy, would serve coffee or lemon water to the guests (who served themselves the rum they dug out from the ground for the event). As she spoke, sometimes the table would move, sometimes the table would rise, sometimes the table would rise and move around.

Whenever he told that tale, Dad would get goosebumps, the hair on his arms standing on end. For Dad, Sanse, the Catholic-Vodou, was very real. So many links to "de-."

I

From Alicia:

When we were young, we would journey west to Manatí— my brothers, Mami, Papá when he was still with us, and me. We would go for the Guanche Festival, celebrations for *la Virgen de la Candelaria*, the one the elders call *Nuestra Señora* or *la Morenita*. Mami would say that we are connected to the Guanches and have been for a very long time, going back to Yuíza, the mother of our line, and her ties to *el Papá Pepe*.

"Here," Mami would say, "we are one with all the people, at home with the Guanche and the few Taíno who keep to the old ways. And we are one with the *libertos* and the runaways like your *papá*, may God rest his soul. Here we are one with all. You and your brothers—Taíno and African of the slaves and African of the Canaries and even European."

She would say these things like a prayer every time we visited Manatí. Then we would ask Mami for a blessing before running off, just like we would before bed. It made her happy. "*Bendiciones, Mami.*" And she would quietly say, "*Que Dios lo' bendiga.*" And then we could run off to enjoy the festival, the processions, the singing and the dancing, the food and playing with the other kids long into the night, an endless family.

I must have been thinking back to those days when I fell asleep last night because I dreamt of *la Morenita* as if she were real, not a statue, but a small gentle woman yet one who radiated power. And though she was dark, *una morenita*, her hair was not brown but light, the color of *pava* straw, and she wore a veil over part of her head, a soft white cloth with a shiny, red lining. And she spoke to me:

"Alicia, *mija*, you live well in Loíza. You and your brothers are honored as of the line of a great *cacica*. But some see you as without respect, failing to love your people. Some say that you disrespect women, not following the ways of the people but going about like a man, a would-be pirate, with those baggy breeches and baggy shirts and that brimless leather hat in this weather, that you try to separate yourself from the people instead of being *of* them."

I could feel my anger even in my dream: "That is so unkind, Señora. I have always dressed like my brothers so that they would never see me as less than them, so that I could scuffle and scrap with them as their equal."

"Yes, of course, and maybe that's how you can be a leader in a world that very quickly changed from the evenness of your Taíno ancestors, those days before women became less than. But not by setting yourself apart from others. You are, after all, no less the child of a former slave than an ancestor of Yuíza and don Pepe. You might not be a slave but neither are you an *hacendida*. Your status extends no further than your home, than Loíza Aldea. And though you might well be *pardo*, you still look black to those who only see white and black, with your beautiful coconut-colored skin and your tight curls, *pelo panal*. You really are, yes, from a line of local royalty. But away from here, the royalty will not show. Besides, with royalty comes responsibility, Alicia."

"Yes. I understand. So what would you have me do?"

"You like to prove you are not weak. But Loíza's people are few in number and not respected by Spain or the *peninsulares* who were born of Spain or even the *criollos*, the Spaniards born on the Island. So I say go to San Juan, child; seek out *el Capitán* don Miguel Enríquez, the *corsario*,[29] and ask to join his crew. He is dedicated to Spain and to the governor, it is true, but he is most of all dedicated to himself. If you can promise him profit, he might well use you while you learn of the world that Loíza is a part of, even as it tries to keep the world at arm's length. Learn of the world, a world of power and wealth that uses our brothers and sisters as domestic beasts or beasts of prey. Be among his pirates. Show him your courage and your desire to fight the enemies of Borikén. Convince him. Be a privateer. And then, with time, decide who the real enemies of the people are. That, I believe, is your destiny, Alicia."

II

Ay, the stuff of dreams. Conversations with the spirit world, eh? What nonsense. I am not even sure that I believe in a spirit world—this mix we have become of the old Taíno ways and Yoruba ways and Christian ways, so many gods like Yúcahu of my mother's line and Olodumare of my father's and Jesucristo of all of us now on pain of death or torture. And so many altars, the *zemis* of the old ways, or the candles of the Mesa Blanca, or the lavish altars of the church. All I am sure of is that we are here, and then we die. It is obvious. It is that simple. Dreams. They are nothing more than conversations with our selves. Scrambled thoughts, or maybe the things we don't want to think about when we are awake.

I mean, when I think about last night's "visitation" I know that it was born of memories of Manatí, all mixed up with the stories from the old men.

The *viejitos* are always spinning tales of other times: stories of the pirate *Pierna de Palo* back when he raided Boríken or at least San Juan, and the pirate Jacques de Sores, a Huguenot who would say he raided because he was angry with Catholics. See what I mean? He raided San Juan, too, and then he went on to cause real damage in *la Habana de Cuba*. And when he raided, he punished the *criollo* landowners not by whipping *them* but by killing their slaves and the few Taíno that remained. Were the slaves Catholic? The Taínos? See? Nonsense. These Huguenot corsairs and the Dutch ones, the other non-Catholic Christians who claimed dedication to the royalty of Normandy or the Dutch: for all their Christian piety, they just killed and sold slaves and the People. Thieves, that's all.

And what of *el viejito* don Rafael who said that his great-grandfather had escaped from the hold of a ship belonging to an English pirate called Francisco el Draque. *El Draque?* The Dragon? We believe anything! And he said that that was the man's real name and he spelled it, D-R-A-K-E, *draque*. Ay, these old men's tales.

They would say that these foreign *corsarios* were heroes to their Lords and Ladies because they captured Spanish goods, like the gold and tobacco Cortés stole from the Maya. The royalty and the elite of their countries could see them as loyal, when all they were really loyal to was the gold and wonders they stole and then shared with the royalty so as not be treated like the sea thieves they are.

It was this—these stories and memories—*these* are what visited me in my sleep, not a ghost or a goddess. I mean, join the crew of Miguel Enríquez? Talk about nonsense. Just a dream, *fantasías*, nothing more.

III

So here I sat, looking out at the clear water, thinking of such things, when a woman came up to me almost out of nowhere. She was just here, and I got this feeling that I should know her. We are not a large community here in Loíza, after all. She was dressed like most, with the long white skirt over bare feet, the white pullover with sleeves rolled up over the elbows. And even though her headwrap was a bit different, a thick red cloth, wrapped high on the head, it was still familiar. Some of those who hold onto African ways still wear the high head-wrap. Yet there was something else. She was not African, not even as dark as I am. She appeared *India*, but I could not make out if she was Taíno or not. Something different, with small scars on her cheeks and nose. And her eyes, so bright.

"*Hola, negrita*, Where is your mind?"

"Just wandering, Señora. Maybe thinking of what lies ahead, out there in the sea. Thinking of the pirates, if you can believe that. And you?"

"Oh, my head is in a whirl from my own traveling. I just came from New Spain. I went and learned so much, like a journey through time. I even learned to read the writings found in Tenochtitlan. And then I decided to learn the language of the friars, the Latin of the Church and of the educated Europeans. So many books in this giant house, *la biblioteca*. So many wonders through time and place."

"*Soy celosa*, Señora, deeply jealous. How did you do that? I mean no disrespect, Señora, but what you describe is not for those like us. As much as I would have liked to go to the grammar school, I could not, for obvious reasons. It was Mami taught me to read. She learned from some good friar."

"Well, I was fortunate. The Maya, you see, were not at peace among themselves like the Taíno tended to be. Many, for that matter, joined with the conquistadors against others of their kind— not traitors as much as collaborators. They thought that working with the Spaniards would help rid the Maya of their enemies. They became the elite Maya who enjoyed the benefits of their adoption of many of the Spanish ways. Some became, in effect, *encomenderos Indios* who could even use other *Indios* as workers, though most of these Maya were kinder to their *Indio* workers than the Invaders are. Some women, *encomenderas-de-Indios*, took me in and treated me as a special guest, including granting me permission to enter *la biblioteca*."

"Ay, how interesting, Señora."

"So when you mentioned pirates, you just reminded me of things I learned about women and the pirates."

"Yes, Señora?"

"I like the respect, señorita, but call me Bushika. And what shall I call you?"

"Alicia. I am Alicia Apolinares y Mejía."

So we talked, and she told me of faraway places in faraway times, and the word *empire*, and how the world has long been places of battling empires, how the Taíno were more the exception when they did not rule by force, keeping their rule through the power of persuasion, convincing the ones ruled that they are better off being ruled than not. And she said that some ancient peoples that she called *Griegos* called this kind of persuasion *hēgemonia*.[30]

But of course, Bushika could see that I did not understand, not really. So she continued.

"Do you not ever wonder, Alicia, how these Europeans manage to control us from across the Ocean Sea? Their numbers here are few, and their rulers are months away by sea! What is their power? That is all I am trying to explain. There is the power of their weapons and their willingness to use them, of course, but there is something else, something beyond the threat of violence, ideas that convince us all—well, most of us—of their superiority, that we can live better than we ever have if we comply, concede. And we believe that our lives might be better if we consent to their rule, even as our lives keep getting worse. If we come to believe that better lives can be gained by riches and that we all have the potential to gain riches, then we have no reason to rebel but to work harder to be more like them or to learn more from them, those who have the riches. And when we fail, we are taught to believe that we are the cause of our own failure. And in order to hold onto those beliefs, we see the few who began like us yet did manage to grow wealthy. The lure of the pirates as corsairs is that they are compliance tied to rebellion. They seem to resist, yet they become rich. That is all I'm trying to say.

"The pirates show that there are other kinds of defiance and other kinds of compliance and even ways of profiting in the process. And those other ways are in taking advantage of situations to aid one side or another but mainly to take care of oneself. Privateering.

"What might be important to you is that I discovered in my readings that the tales we hear of superstitious pirates believing that women on ships bring bad luck is not quite right. It's the men's stereotypes of "ladies" and how the men behave around them. But we are not all "ladies," are we? This takes me back to hegemony, *hēgemonia.* We are told that women are necessarily weak and needing care from men, yet look at Yuíza or Anacaona before her, or the queen Isabel, or the queen of England, Elizabeth, who was the power behind the pirate Francis Drake?"

"Wait! There really was a Francisco el Draque?"

"Very much so. But the point is that as much as we have seen and have known of women as rulers, as powerful, even ruthless, we have come to accept the idea that women are somehow less than men. But women who would dress no different from the men and fight like the men or even better than the men have always been accepted, have even been leaders among pirates, going back to those ancient times of the Greeks I just mentioned, or so the stories go.[31]

"For example, the Greeks fought many a war against a group called the Persians. The Persians were clearly the stronger—except on the seas. But a woman, Artemisia of Caria, literally changed the tide of the sea-wars. In a famous sea battle, the Persian Artemisia lowered the Persian flag from the mast of her ship and replaced it with an Athenian flag. And because she had done that, she was able to get close enough to the Greek vessels to destroy them. So now, when some seek to cause trouble for others by pretending to be the others, it is called a 'false flag' strategy. And since Artemisia was not quite honest in her strategy, at least in terms of 'rules of war,' if there really can be such a thing, then we can say that in some sense she was a woman pirate, 500 years before the birth of Jesús. And there have been many others, like the women from lands far north of Spain, like Alfhild, a shieldmaiden, meaning a woman warrior; she commanded a whole fleet of women pirates."

"I had no idea. I only know of Mary Read and Ann Bonny. I thought they were the only ones."

"Yes, of course. They are the ones who are most visible right now. There is no reason you cannot be just as well known, if you so choose. But as the war among the Europeans about who will rule Spain seems to be coming to an end, the time of the pirates might soon end. So you would need to act quickly, then, should you choose to act."

"But all I said was that I was thinking of such things. Why would you assume I would wish to be a pirate?"

"A guess."

I must have turned away for a moment, because just like that she was gone. After that wonderful conversation, which was longer than I say here, I returned home to tell my brothers and Mami that I was going to San Juan for a while, but that I'd be back. They simply accepted.

IV

So I went to San Juan to find the famous *Capitán*. All seemed to know who he was, but no one could tell me where he might be found. So after a long day searching for the corsair, I needed to rest, and to rest where *una negrita* like me wouldn't call attention, which meant going to the Perla district. And even there, I kept asking after don Miguel while I looked for an inn that would accept me for a price. Then I saw this toothless old fellow with bright eyes and the hint of a smile who heard me asking. And he said:

"We know he is a wealthy man, this *capitán*. And we know, too, that he owns and trades slaves. Unforgivable. But we still accept him here in la Perla when it is time for him to be just a tired mulatto in plain clothes instead of royal corsair. For all his wealth, he has nowhere else to go—only here or the church or maybe the village of Loíza. That's it. So if you travel by the slaughterhouse—your nose will tell you where that is—you will come to an inn, la Cabeza de Cerdo, and there you might also find the man you seek."

V

An Aside. Thoughts from the Spirit Bushika

There will come a time when the Capitán's complexion will be described as "café con leche," a very light brown, lighter than many of the former Andalusians on the Island. Boricuas had sincerely, earnestly embraced las tres razas—European, African, the People—and they will continue to embrace the three long into the future. But the three aren't simply three, nor has power ever been equally divided among the three. When "race" began to change from religion or bloodline to physical features, "European" became complicated in terms of complexion. The power nexus of Puerto Rico continued to be defined by the king in Spain, so that those in power tended to come from Castilla or León and might well have been seen as having "fair skin," but the greatest number of Europeans to the Island came from Andalusia, the final concentration of Moors.

The peninsulare with fair skin was not quite the fairer skin of the Northern Europeans, and Africa is so very large. In Borikén, the Africans were the bozales, who knew nothing of Christian ways, and the ladinos, Christian and Spanish-speaking Africans. And when the king Carlos Segundo sought to increase the population of Borikén as the Taíno who remained on the Island kept dying of guns, germs, slavery, or suicide, Carlos granted parcels of Borikéño land to voluntary residents. These were the vecinos.[32] Most came from the Canary Islands, not the image that comes to mind with the word "African." The people of the Canary Islands were from Europe and Africa, and many were Guanches, their origin unknown. As for the People, the Taíno, they came from afar, from other peoples, not all looking alike when they began the journey north, even if they did eventually form something of a common look, a visual culture. Europe, Africa, the Antilles. Three places of origin, perhaps, but more than three races in how race will come to be described.

So it was and is that the Boricuas claim las tres razas with pride and in earnest but still make distinctions based on surface features: blanco, negro, rojo, amarillo, prieto, trigueño, café con leche, and more. As for those in power, if they could not "see" a clear black, white, or Indian, then mestizo, mulato, or pardo, even when, say, "pure" Guanche. And there was an obvious hierarchy, with those born on the peninsula, los peninsulares, at the top followed by the "pureblood" born in the New World, los criollos, even as la limpieza de sangre had passed.[33]

So this man, this man of café-con-leche complexion, was seen as mulatto by the military head of the Island, Gabriel Gutiérrez de Riva, "el Terrible." His mission was to stop the piracy that was taking an economic toll not only on the Island but on all the king's territories in the Americas. And though Borikén did not provide much mineral wealth, none worth speaking of, really, it did represent the gateway to the

51

Caribbean and the continent. Puerto Rico was "the key to the Indies." So Gutiérrez de Riva thought to fight fire with fire and commissioned a pirate to stop the pirates. But knowing that this was a risky strategy, this hiring a thief against thieves, he thought to appoint a mulatto to head the effort. If the strategy failed, he could just blame what his peers and superiors alike would agree was the inherently unreliable nature of a man who was part African.

Now, loyalty and the letter of the law can be tricky to negotiate, especially when money is involved. Borikén's place in world trade had long ago been limited by King Fernando, when he decided that the Island could only trade with Sevilla. So sugar cane was shipped to Sevilla, but then the River Guadalquivir flooded, and then came the Plague. Sevilla was devastated. No more imported sugar, just local beet sugar. Over time, Borikén disregarded the will of the empire and began bartering with the other colonies, including the British, Dutch, and French on the sea and the French colonies of the mainland. And illicit trade leads to illicit trade—the rise of the pirates. Spain created flotillas to protect traders and used galleon ships so that more of the goods of trade could be carried on larger ships, but all that was expensive and particularly hard for Borikén. Spain could not afford to keep that up, that kind of protection beyond New Spain or Panama. So Spain decided that the Island's economy would require different safety measures, a coast guard. But without money, who would finance a coast guard? The solution? Corsairs, privateers, who would assure the profits of the Island and the empire for a percentage of money "protected" or "acquired."

By the time Alicia met with don Miguel in 1717, he was already an international presence, wealthy, a landowner, a slave owner—though no less mulatto.

As he sat quietly at the inn Cabeza de Cerdo, he seemed to be contemplating the challenges ahead. Still, for all his internal distractions, the unconventionally-dressed young woman got his attention.

VI

"With your permission, don Miguel, may I speak with you?"

And don Miguel gestures for me to sit at his table:

"A thousand thanks, Señor. I am Alicia Apolinares y Mejía of Loíza."

"Ah, the *Mulata* Princess of Loíza, eh?"

"Ay, Señor, you joke. But it is true, and I've been told that I have responsibilities to the people of Loíza. The problem that I see is that I have never been to school and have never traveled beyond the Island. I have hardly even traveled the Island. That is why I am here, to ask if you would allow me to be a member of your crew so that I can learn more of the world."

"*Bueno-o-o.*" He's about to say no, I know.

"Wait! Hear me out before you decide, Señor, please.

"I promise you that I can fight as well as any of your men and would seek no special treatment as a woman. As far as distractions, I am not drawn to women romantically or sexually, so I would not upset the balance among the women on your crews. And as to men, I could never love a man who would wish to rule me, and I could never respect a man I could rule. Whatever is in store for me along the lines of love and romance, they are not for now. I have no patience for it."

I am surprised by the sudden burst of laughter that surrounds me. I was dead serious. And one of the men, seated in the next table says something like, "Oh, this one! I can see her with us, if she is as she says, one who can fight with us and work the muck with us, man the rigging or shit like we do, in plain view atop the bow, the poop deck."

Don Miguel raises his eyebrows and tilts his head at me. He is asking if I can do as the one has said.

I smile: "*Sí. ¿Como no?*"

"Then," says don Miguel, "seeing as you have won the curiosity of the men, yes, you can sail with us aboard my sloop. But the second you become a nuisance, you will be tossed overboard, no matter if we are in the middle of the sea. Understood?"

I become a *corsaria*, accepted among the men. And in quiet times, I learned of my captain. Gossip aboard ship or sitting at a tavern.

Guapo, the bright eyed one with all his teeth and usually brushed hair, tells me that he thinks that the captain is much older than most of us, maybe 40 or 45, that he had to struggle since he was a boy, only able to claim his mother's name because he never knew his father's.

Goyo, a small fellow, even smaller than I am, chimes in, "*E' como es*. His mother was one of the slaves of Leonor Enríquez, we're told. What's interesting, though," he says looking around like it's a secret, "is that this *mulato* from poverty who is our captain is said to know Latin, even had Latin books as a child. So his *papá* was surely a priest, no? After all, how did he learn to read and write? And Latin?"

Chacho Calvo, the beardless bald one keeps up the stage whisper: "People say that the Church has always watched over him, even before he made his own connections to the bishops and such. The Church was there when he first got arrested as a boy. It will always be there for him. You'll see."

Over time I learn of my captain, the mulatto who was knighted a *Caballero* by the king, Felipe Cinco, declared a "don" on all documents, even if still no more than a mulatto to the elites who would never think to address him as "don Miguel," official royal declaration or not, the mulatto who reads Latin, the shoemaker-turned-artillery gunner of the Elite Garrison Corps after being arrested for selling contraband. Don Miguel, *Caballero*, Captain of the Seas and War and Chief Provider to the Crown Corsairs. Quite a force, he. He was even a benefactor of the government, he once told me, providing the governor and the treasurer sizeable loans for the good of Borikén. He, the force that stopped an attempted British invasion and who continues to stop attempts by Denmark and the Dutch.

As for me? I am a pirate, ruthless when necessary. I even became captain of the fleet for a time, when the governor, Francisco Danío Granados, arrested my captain for aiding sick and poor "foreigners," the people of the other islands. And he was accused of being a smuggler. A pirate who is a smuggler? Say not so! But we all knew the arrest had to do with don Miguel not lending money to the treasurer, José Pozo Oneto. Ay, such arrogance from a mulatto to deny his superior in every way. But then Daník's successor, *el Capitán* José Antonio de Medizábal, ordered *Daník's* arrest and ordered that my captain be released.

Over time, I see Trinidad, Margarita, Cumaná, Maracaibo, take part in the trading of slaves from Jamaica, St. Thomas, and Curaçao, trying but failing to remain as emotionally disconnected as don Miguel appeared to be; but these slaves were no different from the people of my home. I could not be indifferent. And we travel to Cádiz, and to Santa Cruz de Tenerife on the Canary Islands, where I hope to meet "real" Guanches, but all I meet are other privateers from the Mediterranean and even a few from the Orient, all of them drinking and carousing. And I take part, at least in the drunkenness, trying to drown out thoughts of those I slaughtered, the dismemberments, or the sight of watching enemies and friends alike choosing to jump overboard, choosing to drown rather than live without a limb, unable to suffer further. I know I will be haunted. And along the way I know I will have to believe in an afterlife, as I see soul after soul leave the eyes of the slaughtered.

VII

Another Aside. Let me, Bushika, the Memory of the People, tell you what I saw.

So it was that on a mission to Veracruz, Alicia left don Miguel's crew, now a wealthy woman. After a hot bath and new clothes—including Turkish women's slacks that she discovered in Northern Africa—she ventured to find the library she heard of so long ago. She traveled the 280 kilometers directly east from Veracruz, mainly walking, sometimes hitching a ride on a passerby's cart, arriving in Ciudad Puebla three days later, quietly entering the Biblioteca Palafoxiana *and its thousands of books, three shelves high down long rooms, vaulted ceilings, an internal city of dark wood and books.*

She sits at one of the reading tables and quietly thinks through how to proceed, where to begin, what the goal is beyond learning. But she decides that learning is enough of a goal for now.

So she wanders, and as she wanders, her eye is drawn to a particular doorway, its frame an elaborate work of carved wood. She enters. She discovers what is called la *Sala Lúdica*, an enclave for children, books in Spanish instead of Latin. She begins here, eventually coming across books on how to read Latin.

She rents a room at the nearby *Posada del Jardín*, beginning her mornings by reading la Gazeta de México over pan dulce y café. Then to the library, stopping at some point for something more to eat from some street vendor or other until it is time to return to the inn for the night. Days at the library begin by learning Latin, sitting beside pensive young boys fascinated by this Black woman in strange slacks, boys who test one another's Latin among themselves. After a while, they include Alicia. Over a few years, she goes from Latin to Greek to Arabic, the language roots of Andalucía, and then to discover the richness of theology.

One series of books especially catches her attention because the title seems not to fit her sense of theology—Suma de Tratos y Contratos (A Manual of Deals and Contracts), written by Fray Tomás de Mercado. It is a kind of practical morality, the morality of money, monopolies, money lending, and trade with and within the New World. And in keeping with earthly things, the writing has an earthly quality, not written in the language of the Latin Scholastics of theology but in Spanish, the language of merchants and bankers, but what really captures her imagination is what Fray Tomás has to say about slavery.

Instead of simply declaring slavery an evil, he weighs different considerations of slavery. His focus is on the black slaves, the ones transported to the Americas, because this brand of slavery extends beyond what he describes as some sort of just and legal slavery. It is reasonable, she reads, that losers in war would serve time as slaves or that those found guilty of a crime would serve time in slavery; it is even reasonable that parents trying to survive would sell a child. This, she reads, is common, a matter of international law, even if not practiced among Christians.

But the acquisition of African slaves for the New World runs into moral problems. First, were the slaves properly enslaved? That is, were they the losers in war, or criminals, or children "rightly" sold by their parents? All too obviously, that is not the case, since Ethiopians, the people of Africa, captured others to sell to the Portuguese and Castilians and others. And that being the case brings the second problem, those who purchased from someone who is not the rightful owner takes part in *the theft and cannot claim rightful ownership. To purchase that which was illegally obtained is to take part in the illegality. And, finally, legally obtained slaves must, morally, have the hope of gaining freedom and returning to their homeland. But those in the New World would have no such hope. So despite the legality under civil law, the slavery of Africans is not legal under natural law, and given the conditions of civil law—war, crime, parental sale—the same would also be true for the* Indios, *since even the freedom to return home cannot be if home becomes the property of the slave owner. In the end, she reads, those who deal in slaves gained outside the boundaries of natural law are doomed to lose their prosperity, since it displeases God so that God punishes them.*[34]

VIII

I had read *La Suma de Tratos y Contratos* back in 1735. It troubled my thoughts about my mentor, don Miguel. He was kind to me and fair to all his crew, but he had been a trader in African slaves, an owner of slaves, even as some part of him was no less a part of Africa. Then, while reading *la Gazeta* one morning, I learned that the governor of Borikén, a Matías de Abadía, had decided to end all dealings with privateers. Don Miguel, it would seem, had not been able to influence this governor. It made me wonder what would become of my pirate *patrón*, but I put that aside and continued my studies.

Five years later, I returned to Loíza. Public grammar schools were few, and what few there were were at the centers of commerce, funded by the *criollos* for their children. Other schools had been opened by local priests, but there weren't many, fewer than twenty priests for the entire island, and their funding had dwindled. So I took my wealth and my learning and opened a school for the children of Loíza. I did it for the people, for *my* people. If they wondered or knew how I had gathered my wealth, the people said nothing.

Now, in those days, news still traveled by word of mouth on the Island. There was no gazette, so it was some time before I heard that don Miguel was living in poverty in the Convent of Santo Tomás de Aquino in San Juan, having been sued by the governor and abandoned by Madrid. It was 1744 by the time I found out. In the next month, February, I would normally join my brothers and their families for the Festival for la Morena at Manatí, but this year, I decided I would take the time to visit my old master of the seas.

That night I dreamed with *la Morenita*. The last time was so very long ago. This time, she was not alone but was with an *India*, not Taíno, with hair cut like some of the *Indias* I met in Cumaná, but with sticks in her cheeks and through her nose, wearing nothing more than a long red cloth that hung from her waist to her knees. And I wondered why she seemed familiar; wondered, that is, until she smiled. Then I knew it was la Señora Bushika, the woman by the beach, not having aged as I had.

The moment I recognized Bushika, *la Morenita* faded from view, and Bushika raised a finger, pointing to her ear, telling me to listen. And what I heard was a male voice, a very familiar voice:

"*¡Mira la Princesa Mulata!*"

Don Miguel! I heard his ready laughter.

"My time among the living ended not long ago, and so I am here, near the Memory of the People, Bushika, but I cannot be *among* the People. It is true that we are all forgiven for our sins, but to forgive is not to reward, so I remain near but never among, to be removed from the records of history for two hundred years to come. But you, Alicia, you do not have to share in my fate, do not have to be as isolated in death or life as I was during my last years, as isolated as I will remain through eternity. Now, you, you were as kind to me as you were loyal, even as I could easily see that you did not approve of so many of my ways. I always saw that. You never said that I had betrayed my people for some power and for money—that I had betrayed them for a respect I was never to gain, not from Madrid, not from the *criollos*, not from the *gente*. Yet approve or not, you were a mighty warrior, for which you were rewarded. And now you do some good with your earnings and using your learning for the People.

"But the mind is not enough, Alicia. You heard the spirits even as you denied their reality. Not everyone can speak to and visit with those of the spirit, Alicia. This is a gift. All that you heard from the spirits, all that you obeyed and fulfilled, were for a purpose, to be a doorway for those who need more than the blessings of the priests, as wonderful and wonderous as they might be. It is you, you who must lead our People, not only by way of the intellect but through the heart, the soul. You are blessed, and may God continue to bless you."

And as I awoke, I knew this time the dream was a Vision, even as don Miguel was not allowed to be visually present.

IX

Bushika:

The morning after don Miguel and I had visited with Alicia, the parents who normally sat in her classroom with the children seemed to sense that something was different in Alicia. As they listened to doña Alicia they felt their hearts swell. They knew, and as they left the classroom that morning, they bowed and sought to kiss the ring she wore, a ring she had had since she was a child attending Festival, a cameo of la Morenita, but Alicia would not allow it. Instead, from that day forward, she wrapped a rosary around her hand, so that those who would kiss her ring would instead kiss the crucifix on the rosary.

And because the priests were few, showing up on distant occasions, Alicia became the spiritual advisor of the village, the one who people knew could speak with the dead as they left the one world to join the other. Alicia became the local espiritualisma and became known as Mama Alicia as she aged. She lived a long life, ninety-eight years, dying in her sleep in 1798 as respected among the regional clergy as she was among the people.

5 From Clara's Journal
alloiōsis [35]

Dad would speak of the young man who dated his sister. The young man had black wavy hair and a good physique (both mattered to Dad, wavy hair and a good physique), and the young man loved the Island. The U.S. government had finally figured out that the men who walked around wearing black guayaberas, *the loose-fitting shirts of the tropics, were revolutionaries, members of the Nationalist Party of Puerto Rico led by Dr. Pedro Albizu Campos,* el Maestro, *the Teacher.*

The young man had run into the tropical rainforest, el Yunque, *where Dad, himself a boy, would take the young man dry clothes and food every day. I don't know the story beyond that. Dad would always go on to lament that his sister married someone else.*

For a very long time I thought Dad disliked his brother-in-law, Tito Santana, because he was Black (the mentality of the boy from Brooklyn), but I learned that Tito's race was never the issue with Dad. His problem with tío Tito was that he was a gambler and a drinker (though he was the one who treated me best as an English-dominant boy in Puerto Rico in 1958). Tito was "less than" his sister's former suitor. Tito was not serious, not the revolutionary, not a man of dignity, as far as Dad was concerned.

Dad, the revolutionary in his heart.

The day before Dad died, I asked what Tito's last name was. It had been nearly 50 years since I had been with tío Tito and titi Margarita, Dad's sister, in Puerto Rico.

Dad said, "Santana." Then more to himself, he said, "I thought he was Puerto Rican."

Confused, I said, "Tito?"

"No. Carlos."

Dad, was a singer, one who even managed a gig on Ted Mack and the Original Amateur Hour *on TV before we even owned our own TV, and Dad managed some NYC nightclub gigs, knowing that the entertainment business and sports were all that was open to the Other (my phrase, not his; his was simply "us"). So he wanted to see Carlos Santana as something of a Puerto Rican icon, the one who made it big (since some of his tunes are Puerto Rican tunes, like Tito Puente's* Oye Como Va*). But no, Santana is not a Puerto Rican. I felt the need to say "I'm sorry, Dad," but didn't.*

Carlina writes:

19 de Diciembre 1901

Our family has always been gifted with long lives, thanks be to God. My great aunt Alicia, who I only knew through the stories my father told and the tales others told, died at the age of 98. I was born two years later, in the year of Our Lord 1800. And now, as I write this with a steady hand by the grace of God and a lovely Waterman pen, I am one-hundred-and-one-years-old, looking into the new century and the new ruler of my home, my Borikén, even as the new ruler won't even say "Puerto Rico," never mind "Borikén." But home will always be Borikén, all that is left from the time before the Invaders and the Invaders of the Invaders.

One hundred and one, and a life, I know, no different from the lives of all of us who live as long. My life has known love won and love lost, joy and sorrow, the joy of a lifetime lover, the grief of having my lover taken from my side. And I have played with grandchildren and great-grandchildren and have buried children at birth, God calling them to Him when I thought I would have so much time or having had them yanked from my hand by the winds of another hurricane. I have feared dying of tears and have laughed to tears. I have wondered at the rulers and at their rulers, we who obeyed and those who rebelled, watched Time tell tales of irony and contradiction. But Loíza remains. Some tried to claim her, the French and the Hessians and the English, but we remain, still home to former slaves, *libertos*, mulattos, and the few who try against all odds to hold onto Taíno ways. In my early years, I read of the world through letters from my father. He had traveled to Europe, after my mother died trying to bring forth another child. I also heard of our world on the Island from the workers of the fields and the workers in the *haciendas* when they would sit in my kitchen over *café con pan sobao*. And, like all of us, I have always known that my time is limited. Every night I pray that this land I love will someday be free.

***

Long ago, when I was 16, my father decided to go to France to earn a degree so that he could open a college in Loíza.

Why France? Why not Salemanca?

He said because when one is in Spain these days, one is already in France. Besides, he had heard that Napoleón had changed what colleges look like in interesting and important ways.

I remember. I remember that Papá said what others were saying. It was the feeling of the time about France in Spain. It was that feeling, that *la Madre Patria*, Spain, was lost. I know that Spain was a harsh mother, but she is what we became, *tres razas* and all. Still, I could never truly understand how or why so many of the wars for independence among our neighbors del Sur were as much fought *for* Spain than against her. She had betrayed them, I guess. My father would shake his head and mutter that Spain hadn't been Spain in so very long, at least had not been fully of Spain. Even though France was ruling Spain in those days, France was simply just another new ruler, another from so many since the days of Isabela and Fernando. After the Catholic Monarch, Juana la Loca, married Felipe el Hermoso, Spain became Habsburg, the Spain of Austria. Even so, these were still seen as Spain's glory days, when don Felipe el Prudente, King Felipe Segundo, moved the center of Spain to Madrid and ruled so much of Europe: Portugal, Naples, Sicily, England, and Ireland. Well, England not for very long, only as long as Felipe's marriage to Bloody Mary, who died young. Don Felipe was also the Duke of Milan and Lord of the Seventeen Provinces of the Netherlands, and king of the Spanish colonies, ocean to ocean, with islands named after him, *las Filipinas*. This was the Spain of even the colonized's dreams, the golden age of a truly powerful Spain. And maybe Felipe Tercero and Felipe Cuarto were not great regals, but Spain remained, even if still a part of the

House of Habsburg. And then came Carlos Segundo, the Bewitched one, not well of the head and remaining childless, and the War of Succession that my aunt Alicia-the-Corsair had taken part in during her pirate days. No more Habsburg. Don Felipe el Quinto is king. But then comes Napoleón, and the Spanish empire folds. Even as it doesn't. Even as it does. I mean, even though Napoleón seats his brother José as the king of Spain and, later, Fernando el Sexto abdicates the throne to France for a time, Spain and its kings continued to rule—to own—us, the colonies of this part of the world. She was our ruler, even as she was a puppet of Napoleón.

Oh, the revolutions. What is interesting to me was (did I write it already?) . . . Interesting is that the revolutions were more about France than about true independence. There were those who wished true independence, like Simón Bolívar, of course, yet the citizens, as opposed to the gentry like don Simón, seemed resigned to remain with Spain, but a free Spain, a Spain that was no one's puppet. Then again, who were the "citizens" when one is a colony that owns slaves and indentured workers who never had a say? I guess when I write "citizens," I could just well write *criollos*.

And why would the *criollos* wish for revolution, after all? Revolutions are fought when there is nothing left to lose. For every humanitarian gesture by Spain or the *peninsulares* appointed to govern or the Borikén-born *criollo* appointees, there was a counter that assured that power and profit would more or less remain the same. And when the Taíno were freed from the *encomienda*, they were made to forfeit their customary clothing and made to receive baptism. So the Taíno mixed with the Spanish and the Africans, like the Mother of Loíza Aldea had done so long ago. The Taíno were eliminated through adaptation—through assimilation—more effectively than they had been through slaughters or disease. They were assimilated to near-death. My father would call the *jíbaros*, the county folk, "*los restos*," the remnants of the Taíno. Mere remnants.

So the Taíno-as-*jíbaros* were freed and then subject to subsistence or to selling the foods they grew or other kinds of barter, or they became laborers. As for the slaves, they were freed only to become laborers, too, forced to find jobs, forced to carry *libretas*, the papers to prove they were not vagrants. If they couldn't find work, they were sent to jail or forced into municipal work for half-pay. Unless "revolution" meant the end of the powerful, the end of plantation owners, the end of those who could take part in international trade, the laborers would not see an end to their labors. What kind of freedom is that?

As for the *criollos*, they had plenty to lose if there were a true revolution. So those of this part of the world who "belonged" to Spain tried to force out France, and they lost. France was too powerful. There was nothing left to do, then, other than to create their own Spanish-American "kingdoms." That was their independence, but Cuba and Borikén would not take part.

I know I make a string out of what is really a web, that I make the complicated simple. So much to tell; so little time left in this world, I know. I wish only to point to the way it was. Like when I was sixty-five or seventy, somewhere along there, when Spain decided to re-colonize Santo Domingo. We heard of the war in Santo Domingo, a war not carried out in battlefields, but guerrilla wars, just like the little wars Spain was attempting against the French at the same time that Spain was also busy fighting off Cuban slave rebellions and other rebellions in Peru or Chile. But while all that was going on, Boricuas, like don Segundo Ruiz Belvis and José Julián Acosta, were in Madrid, talking, reasoning, arguing that abolishing slavery would not have to hurt the Cuban and Boriqueño economies. It was always about the money. Eventually, the Spaniards were persuaded that they could make the grand gesture of freeing the slaves as long as the economy remained stable. Spain took her time to make the change, but she did.

So don Segundo, when he returned to the Island, gathered together our leaders, and he decided to include don Ramón Betances y Alacán, the mulatto physician. A good man, don Ramón. When his father became a landowner in Hormigueros, it was don Ramón who convinced his father to free his small group of slaves. And when we were hit by the cholera, it was don Ramón and his friend Dr. José Francisco Basora who cared for the sick and opened a hospital. A good man, don Ramón, who died just the other day, it seems, died somewhere in France, where he was a diplomat in the service of Cuba and Santo Domingo. He could not be a diplomat for us because he tried to lead a revolt, *El Grito de Lares*, the great revolt. At least it was supposed to be great, but don Rámon had been betrayed, so the rebellion never took place, so he was sentenced to permanent exile. Still, don Ramón showed that rebellion was possible, even in a Borikén loyal to Spain.

I have lived through a century of revolution, the century when Spain's imperial greatness was diminished, if not demolished. And I saw Puerto Rico, my Borikén, gain its independence on the 25th of November 1897, when the Spanish parliament issued *la Carta Autonómica*. Spain would continue to represent us internationally, but we would have our own government.

That happened in February 1898. Our first legislative session was scheduled for March. Then it was postponed because the United States had just declared war against Spain. The Spanish in Cuba had blown up one of the U.S.'s ships, the *Maine*, killing all on board. That is what the world was told, but we knew different. We saw the ship explode from the inside. A furnace explosion was more likely than an attack from Cuba.[36] It was how to get the people of the United States to sanction a war so that that country could take the Spanish colonies of the Caribbean and the Pacific. That was April 1898. Such an easy year to remember, 1898. That July, the United States became our new owner, even if not officially until 10 December of that year. None of us, no Boricuas, took part in the Paris peace treaty that would decide our fate. And as long as they were negotiating, the U.S. purchased the Philippine Islands and Guam. Cuba and Borikén were just cards in a game, and the autonomy that never was was lost.

The new Authority was General John Brooke at first, and then General Guy Henry. But even before General Guy, General John ended all elections and made education in English mandatory, of course. In the same way Spain had cut out the Taíno tongue, the U.S. began its own surgery. And just as Borikén had become San Juan Bautista and then Puerto Rico, Puerto Rico would now be *Porto Rico*, officially declared in October, even before the Treaty. Still, the poor joyfully greeted the "Americans" as the Spaniards departed.[37] Then General Henry did away with the Autonomous Council, and the government became solely American.

***

Papá never did build a college. He lived out his years as a well-respected teacher in the school that my great aunt created. But there was a new school for the island in Fajarda in 1900, a Normal School, *la Escuela Normal Industrial.* I believe an even better school will grow from that.

In 1901, the Supreme Court of the U.S. settled a lawsuit brought by a Downes & Company who wanted their import tax money back, taxes they had paid for a shipment of oranges that went from here to New York. The company argued that there was no import, that the shipment had been within the U.S. After all, Porto Rico was a part of the U.S. The Court said no. One of the Supreme Court men, a Justice Edward Douglas White, wrote that "whilst in an international sense Porto Rico was not a foreign country, since it was subject to the sovereignty of and was owned by the United States, it was foreign to the United States in a domestic sense, because the island had not been incorporated into the United States, but was merely appurtenant thereto as a possession."[38] My English is not good, so this never made sense to me. Another Justice, Henry Billings Brown, wrote that though "the annexation of distant possessions is desirable," our island is "inhabited by alien races, differing from us in religion, customs, laws, methods of taxation, and modes of thought."[39] I read this in our newspaper. I had to wonder what this judge imagined us to be. This was the same court, though, I was told, that decided that Black Americans would be equal to others as long as they did not mix with them. That, at least, is the best I can make of "separate but equal." Puerto Rico was not even *that* fortunate. We would be separate *and* unequal.

***

In the Name of God, I must stop here. I have to. I need to put down my beautiful pen and let go of the politics as best I can. I know it is time just to watch the world from my kitchen, enjoy bread and coffee with those who come to see if I am still alive, and continue to enjoy gazing at the wonder of the sea from my window.

Fin

***

Bushika from the Record of Time and Memory

Soon after she put down her pen, doña Clara went to sleep only to awake by me in this new-timeless place, looking like she did when she was thirty-five, the dashing don Luís, her lover and husband, by her side, the two of them in the company of kin and loved ones. And I am nearby, continuing to watch the Record of the land founded by the line of my Daví.

Centuries are like the tides, knowing nothing of calendars. So the last remnant of the Age of Revolutions of the 19th century would be a mulatto born in 1891 but remembered for his voice during the 20th century, *el Maestro*, don Pedro Albizu Campos. And seeing how he was, in a sense, the last of the 19th century rebels, I invited doña Clara to join me in exploring the Record.

"Come, look to the frail creature before you, nearly a skeleton, sitting there with a blanket on his lap and a wet towel around his head. That is don Pedro Albizu Campos, not quite the pathetic fellow he appears to be, so much more than 'The King of Towels,' as his jailers with no respect call him. He will soon join us.

"Those towels are to protect him from what he says is a kind of weapon that is as strange as those bird-machines that were created soon after you left the world of flesh. And just like those aeroplanes, the weapon he believed was targeting him was real. He said he was subject to radiation, like beams of invisible light, radio waves like those of the wireless telegraph of your final years, radio waves mixed with the power of a magnet. Yes, it sounds crazy. All doubted when don Pedro said he was being subject to these rays of weaponized light and magnetism, radiation. The people said, 'Poor Dr. Pedro has had a stroke and gone mad.' But he knew such things were theoretically possible and that the experiments were likely.

"So the King of Towels will die soon, honored—and pitied. You know so well, Clara, how quick the young are to question the minds of the old. But he was not crazy. The truth will come out long, long from now.[40]

"And in this time before us, he will be honored in death and memorialized long after. He will be remembered as the revolutionary without a revolution, honored and loved."

And so I continued to show the story of don Pedro, how he had managed a law degree from Harvard despite a poor upbringing after his mother died and his father abandoned him. And how he became a lawyer, one who exposed a man of science, Dr. Cornelius Rhoads, who actually wrote that:

> Porto Ricans . . . are beyond doubt the dirtiest, laziest, most degenerate and thievish race of men ever inhabiting this sphere. What the island needs is not public health work but a tidal wave or something to totally exterminate the population. It might then be livable. I have done my best to further the process of extermination by killing off 8.[41]

Don Pedro exposed him, though nothing came of it—since he, Rhoads, never did kill anyone. But the racism was clear enough. Then don Pedro went on to challenge the giant U.S. sugar industry, Domino Sugar, and won, yet the sugar company continues. For all his efforts, his Nationalist Party could only get four percent of the vote in an election. He was loved but not really followed.

He was a revolutionary *speaker* more than a revolutionary. When two nationalists killed Colonel Francis Riggs, the person many believed responsible for the police's murder of four nationalists and an innocent bystander, don Pedro publicly declared the killers of Riggs—who were executed without trial—martyrs and heroes. And it was that speech that got don Pedro ten years in a U.S. prison, from 1937 to 1947. Three years after he got out of prison, in 1950, nationalists ransacked the home of the first-ever *elected* governor of Puerto Rico, José Luis Muñoz Marín, the first in the entire colonial history of the Island. And while that was happening, other nationalists attacked President Harry Truman at the Blair House in Washington. Don Pedro, as the president of the Nationalist Party, was held responsible and sentenced to eighty years in prison in Puerto Rico, but Governor Muñoz Marín issued a pardon three years later.

This is when don Pedro became the King of Towels.

Then Lolita Lebrón and three others fired weapons into the gallery of the Capitol Building in Washington, wounding some of the politicians. Don Pedro is again blamed, and he's back in jail. Two years later, 1956, he suffers a stroke and is transferred to the Presbyterian Hospital in San Juan, where he stays until Governor Muñoz Marín again pardons him, November 1964. A few months later, in April 1965, he dies.

Pedro Albizu Campos was a political revolutionary, but not an armed revolutionary, not even as active as don Ramón Betances who had tried to bring weapons to the Borikéños. Don Pedro's weapon was rhetoric.

And rhetoric actually was against the law.

Albizu was guilty of breaking the 1948 Law 53, *la Ley de la Mordaza*, a law against speaking out, a law against any speeches that propose independence. It was a law that was revoked nine years later, because if Borikén was subject to U.S. laws, then it was also subject to U.S. protections, including the First Amendment to the U.S. Constitution. But by the time Law 53 was repealed, don Pedro was already back in jail.

So even as it is true that thousands gathered to hear don Pedro speak of independence, and tens of thousands joined his funeral procession, there were no thousands to act on his speeches. [42]

IV

So as I look at the Record, it is clear that there has always been and there will always be attempts at independence. Throughout the twentieth century, there were movements in America's New York, including the very public Young Lords. But most of those who went to New York went there to find work after the U.S. Supreme Court declared in 1904 that "Porto Ricans" were not aliens after all. And even more went to New York after 1917 when the Puerto Ricans were granted citizenship, though they still needed Green Cards, *las Saldañas*, named after M.T. Saldaña, whose signature was on all the cards. So they went, the freedom seekers among the migrants, and they practiced their freedom of speech.

Freedom. Time shows that there is no ideal more basic beyond love than the will to freedom. Yet what does this freedom look like? The great singers of words, the poets, the students and teachers of wisdom, and the philosophers could never truly say what love is; still, everyone, educated or not, a lover of language or not, can recognize love or at least everyone can believe to have known love. But freedom is always just one step away. It is always *right there* but never truly *here*. The ancestors even before me, Bushika, the Keeper of Memory, even before the Arawak or the Taíno, all sought freedom. They searched and searched, and when they found it on the islands of the sea, there were still the Caribes and the hurricanes and new diseases, and then the new conflicts. And when the Europeans' ways became the only way, the People sought freedom from slavery but could not find freedom from bigotry.

So the people choose to accommodate, to find moments of joy, more joy than not, given love and family and all the wonders of life and a belief in the possibility of afterlife. There is joy. But is it freedom, or is it joy despite freedom's lack?

When the Boricuas of the 19th century looked at the freed ones of the rest of the former colonies of Spain, they didn't see a model for true freedom.[43] Economic dependence, and the poor stayed hungry in those independent places, even as they were moved by the passion and the eloquence of great speakers like Simón Bolívar or, later, Albizu Campos.

They hear. They desire. But the majority who are not among the worst off accommodate. This is how hegemony operates: accommodations to maintain consent (and call it *consensus* rather than *concession*). So to elect a governor of Puerto Rico rather than accept an appointed one and be declared *un Estado Libre Asociado*, a "Free Associated State" but translated to English as a commonwealth. The gestures placate not only the Puerto Ricans but the world that watches and knows that its real status remains—officially—an "unincorporated territory," a colony.

6 (Or is it an Epilogue?) The Author Writes of Soqui

metabasis [44]

Who knows how many thousands of times I heard Dad (who was Daddy but never Papá, yet Mom was Mami till adolescence, when she became Mom) begin a sentence with "Mira, Soqui." That mira is the Puerto Rican "hey," a kind of "looky here." The Black folks of the neighborhood would know to get our attention with that: "Hey, mira, mira." But for Dad, it was more the opening to a conversation, maybe the opening to a different point of view that was not an argument. When Mami got aggravated with some boss or other (and other like situations), Dad would begin with, "Calma, Soqui," kind of like take a breath but without condescension (well, none that I could see). This is Mami's story.

They had all come from somewhere, the Boriqeños, traveling the land, paddling the rivers and then the seas so many centuries ago. And they were joined by others from across the ocean: some not by choice and others, the poor seeking better or the wealthy seeking more. Travelling was in the souls, and so it is that the poor Boricuas of the 20th century ventured north, sailing aboard steamships, the *Marine Tiger*, the *Borinquen*, the *Coamo*, heading to New York City, the West Side or the Lower East Side of Manhattan, the Bronx, or Flushing Avenue near the Brooklyn Navy Yard or Williamsburg in Brooklyn. They called their New York communities "*las colonias.*" They had traveled from *the* colony to *a* colony. They knew. Then came relatively inexpensive air travel, Waterman Airlines or Pan American or chartered flights for farm workers. The Great Migration of the late 1940s and 1950s. And some were sold by parents to work as servants for the wealthy of the Upper West Side or the wealthy suburbanites of Chicago and thereby provide for families on the Island. The migrants gave birth to children, born in the U.S., full citizens, prompted to assimilate though assimilating proved easier for those who were white or "olive-skinned" than those the shades of brown, the long-familiar sorting of blacks and whites, a sorting that assured Puerto Rican unification as a reaction, even when never having been to Puerto Rico, even as their Spanish changed in this new world and even as their Spanish would fade, not lost but no longer whole for many of the mid-twentieth-century generation.

II

Soqui was sixteen when she began dating the young soldier, a man five years older than she. The woman who raised her, the one she called Mami, had misgivings about this soldier who would come to the door of the rectory where they lived. Soqui's birth mother had no say in the matter, even as she lived only a block away with Soqui's sister and brothers, those who she watched play but could not join. Soqui had been rejected at birth when her father had been shot to death while in another woman's bed. So a housemaid to the local parish priest volunteered to raise the girl, María Socorro, Socorro, Soqui, and, in raising her, was able to provide her with a parochial school education. But she quit school during her third year of high school. The soldier was blamed, when the cause of her dropping out was a refusal to dissect a frog for a school project. At least, that's the story.

"*Te va a dar la tuberculosis*," "He'll give you tuberculosis." So to save Soqui, her mother sold her (well, "contracted" her) to a wealthy family in Chicago. Her Mami had exchanged three years of service for a substantial fee, enough for Soqui's Mami and new husband to move comfortably to New York. In Chicago, the young woman would be provided a room in the lovely home, an allowance of five dollars a week, a handsome allowance in 1946, and as the one who did the cleaning and the cooking, she would be provided food, though she would have to learn to prepare more typically American meals. She had learned enough English in Puerto Rico during her three years of high school and the years of elementary to make her way through cookbooks and to be accepted as "one of the family," that tired old trope for owning slaves and servants who feed and care for the children.

Besides, Soqui was a charmer, a white Puerto Rican—slender, dark curly hair, a fine nose, relatively full lips, hazel eyes, and a smile that could light the dark. Then, one night, she climbed out the window of her room with a single piece of luggage and made her way to the Greyhound station for a bus to New York, paying the fare with savings from her allowance. And there, in New York, she met up with her soldier. A few weeks later, she turned twenty-one. Two weeks after that, they married. And ten months later, a son, their first child. Times were hard.

A poem: Víctor Villanueva y Hernández[45]

Triste lucha la del árbol con espinas	Sad struggle of the tree of thorns
Fuerte ardor que sólo a su alma se cobija.	Burning that can only take shelter in your soul.
Vano empeño para el ser que vive,	Vain striving for he who lives,
En tratar de comprender su propria vida.	In trying to understand his own life.
Muy dulce es percivir de la noche Sus caricios;	How sweet to feel your caresses in the night;
Pero es terrible saber	But it's so terrible to know
Que mas tarde en la madrugada	That later in the light of day
Agonizando todos ellos quedan. . . .	All the agonies remain. . . .
Triste lucha del árbol con espinas	Sad struggle of the tree of thorns
triste lucha la del que ya un poquito tarde,	sad struggle, that which is already a little late,
Ni siquiera el más leve suspiro	Yet even your lightest sigh

su alma alienta.	encourages the soul.

Triste e interminable lucha	Sad and interminable struggle
esta que jamás se aleja	that which will never leave
¡Oh, que triste lucha ésta	Oh, how sad this struggle
que a mi pecho	Weighing so on my chest!
Tanto apena!	
¡Triste lucha . . . triste lucha!	Sad struggle . . . sad struggle!
--"En el pasado	--"In the past
versa tu presente"	turns the present"
19 de enero 1951	19 January 1951

III

It seemed a lifetime on one city block in Williamsburg, Brooklyn, Bartlett Street. The first apartment was really a converted storefront. Victor (Sr.) painted the large display window in black and hung cloth between the window and the bedroom where they began raising their Victor Jr. Soqui found the place, seeing the "To Let" sign on the storefront window of The Gypsies' fortune-telling business. And then 47 Bartlett, up two flights of stairs, where Victor laid new linoleum and installed a modern sink with a white sheet-metal skirt and doors to hide the pipes. Soqui made friends with the neighbor, the old Jewish woman who would care for their son, their Papi, from time to time. From there to a two-bedroom with even a washing machine at 22 Bartlett, Bartlett Street, a block away from the Pfizer Pharmaceutical's chemical plant and two blocks to All Saints Elementary—sandwiched between faith and capital. And there they stayed until another child, a daughter, came into the world, and they moved to the projects of Bedford-Stuyvesant (which Soqui would pronounce *estewie-vessent*), a step up from the tenements like the projects were intended to be.

And then a breaking of the peace. And New York is in flames.

The New Yorker, 1 August 1964, p. 23

Talk story about the Negro riots which spread from Harlem to the Bedford-Stuyvesant section of Bklyn. What set Bedford-Stuyvesant off, as it had set Harlem off two days before, was the fatal shooting on Jul. 16th of a 15-year-old Negro, James Powell, by a white police lieutenant Thomas Gilligan, in Yorkville. The Bedford-Stuyvesant ghetto is bigger than Harlem, more heavily populated, and tougher. Account of the four-day riots, breakdown of arrests and broken store windows. Attempts at appeal for peace by the NAACP went unheeded, their sound trucks were mobbled and routed. The Reporter was threatened by a group of Negroes but was given a chance to scurry to safety by a Negro youth who distracted the mob.[46]

Victor is caught in the melee as he attempts to get home from his shift as a mechanic for New York Metro, and Papi had gotten caught in a different melee at the vocational high school, Hamilton. And Soqui and Victor had a two-year-old daughter yet to raise.

Soqui decided it was time to leave the city. But rather than move to Queens or the suburbs of Long Island, the new *colonia* for those whose incomes began to approximate a kind of middle class, Soqui or Sophie (her concession to English) decided they would move to California, where Victor's cousin had ended up thanks to the relocation of the cousin's husband, a career military man. So many Boricuas and others would discover new places to live thanks to military relocations. Eventually I, too, would be relocated thanks to the military, relocated to the Pacific Northwest, where I remain a half-century later, and Soqui (or Sophie) and Victor, with daughter in tow, would feel the need to follow their grown son, the undeniable pull of family, the grandchildren. And there they stayed, when age grabbed hold and no longer allowed for yet another move.

IV

Victor on his deathbed in an industrial hospital bed in a cold, ascetic, overly lit room in the hospice wing of the giant VA hospital in Spokane, Washington, slips into a coma, as Soqui, their children, and their grandchildren speak words of love to him, prayers to wing him along on the journey sure to come. A cough, a clenching of teeth, and a tightening of muscles that pull him into a fetal position, and he is gone. So far from home but never not a Puerto Rican. The day before, he had sadly acknowledged that Carlos Santana was not a Puerto Rican.

And soon after, Soqui slides into the long goodbye, lost to a time when she was a teenager on the Island, "waking up" when Victor Jr. and his daughters or with his new mate would come to visit, or when the grandson came by. Soqui, alone in a dingy hospice, the best the children can do. And Victor Jr. must tell the staff in that awful place to call her Soqui, not Sophie. She had returned to the Island in her mind, would no longer know *Sophie*. And she dwindles away in the middle of the Pacific Northwest, soon to dance again with Victor, her *Víctor*. How they danced.

V

This is the way of those who left the Island, when the hope of returning was lost, when the children did become the Americans they had hoped the children would be, even as the children themselves discovered new identities, new representations— Spanish, Hispanics, Latinos and Latinas, Latinx—the different ways of those from the various Spanish colonies whose cultural ways differed, whose Spanishes differed, but who the *Norteños* continue to assume are all somehow the same and never quite fully American but ethnics. But the young ones, the young ones on the Island[47] and throughout the world today remember the Taíno and try to rekindle Boricua ways—ancient and long, long before the Americans were Americans, long before the Taíno became *Indios*.

Endotes

1. My age is showing, I realize. I would prefer "Latinos," but of course I understand the inclusiveness missing in the male suffix. I understand why the -x, but I am nevertheless troubled by the Anglicization of "Latinx," so I turn to the already-existing neuter gender of Spanish, the -e suffix.

2. That first national publication was "Whose Voice Is It Anyway? Rodriguez' Speech in Retrospect" (1987), where I made a distinction between the immigrant and those of us who came to America through colonization, including the colonization of the body which is slavery.

3. What drew me to Fanon should be obvious enough: he, like I was, was a veteran from the colonies who fought for the empire and thereby had to face internal colonialism. It was Fanon who allowed me to see the contradiction. As for Dussel: (1) there was my already established affinity for liberation theology (back when I was a grad student, an affinity which then pulled me into the work of Paolo Freire) reflected in *Philosophy of Liberation* and (2) what I saw as a play on words with his Invention of the Americas, since invention was once synonymous with *discovery.*

4. I use scare quotes in recognizing that "classical rhetoric" is a very narrow conception of the history of rhetoric, since Kenneth Burke (e.g., *A Rhetoric of Motives*, 1969) and others like Paulo Valesio (*Novantiqua: Rhetorics as Contemporary Theory*, 1980) see rhetoric as ontological and thereby having as many histories as there are languages and cultures.

5. Explaining these theorists and their concepts would take me far beyond my intention here, but explanations can be found in my "Hegemony: From an Organically Grown Intellectual (1992) or my "An Introduction to Social Scientific Discussions on Class" (1998).

6.   The philosopher Stephen Toulmin (who used to be invoked in composition textbooks to provide a method of logic for argumentation) decided that discussions on epistemology would be best if they concerned practical applications rather than complex considerations into the natures of perception, memory, consciousness, reason, only to have all those considerations undone by philosophies of skepticism, which ask if knowledge is even knowable. Following Toulmin, then, Richard Scott (1967) writes that the application of the epistemological is through rhetoric. Richard Cherwitz and James Hikins flesh out the question of rhetoric and the epistemological in *Communication and Knowledge* (1986), writing that they "do not claim that language forms a criterion of knowledge, [but that] language is a feature common to all knowledge claims." They go on to say that their "point to be highlighted is that questions of knowledge are bound up with questions of language and its use, which is to say, with *rhetoric* broadly conceived" (21, 41). In other words, even as I accept that in order to de-link from coloniality one must break from Western epistemological universal conceptions, one can't break from that knowledge without giving voice to that from which we are to break. And there's the problem: what we know of our epistemologies is what we say (even as internal monologues) but that is not all that we know. From crib (or before) to tomb we gather knowledge, and not all of it is articulated; most of it enters what Michael Polanyi (1966) terms "the tacit dimension," the knowledge known but tending not to be codified. As I'll try to demonstrate in the fourth chapter, somewhere between the depths of the epistemological and the rising to true critical consciousness lies the ideologies contained within hegemony, what Gramsci calls the "common sense." These commonly held conceptions are carried in language, in the rhetoric of the everyday as betrayed through sociological frames or rhetorical tropes.

7. A literal translation of Aníbal Quijano's "*patrón colonial de poder*" is the colonial pattern of power rather than the "colonial matrix of power" (*un patrón* rather than *una matriz*). The matrix that Mignolo lays out, based on Quijano, is more in keeping with sociological frames, a form of analysis that recognizes tropes in everyday speech, a method developed by Ervin Goffman in *Frame*

Analysis, a method he based on a concept he called "dramaturgy," derived explicitly from Kenneth Burke, a matter I discuss briefly in "Puerto Rico: A Neoliberal Crucible" (2014), also employed in sociologist Eduardo Bonilla-Silva's works exploring "color-blind racism" (2006, 2022). Quijano, after all, is a sociologist. He would, of course, turn to his discipline's methodology. But a pattern rather than a matrix keeps me within my own discipline's discourse, the realm of rhetoric, suggesting tropes and the ideological dimensions contained within tropes. Boaventura DeSousa Santos dedicates most of a chapter of his *Epistemologies of the South* (2016) to what he terms "metonymic reason," the idea that the world supremacy of the West is really a metonymy, insofar as the East and others have never really accepted that supremacy. He also chooses to define *topos*, the commonplace, as "the notion or idea that—because it is self-evident in a given cultural context—is not argued about. On the contrary, it functions as a premise of argumentation" (219n).

8. Why the Greco-Latin? Because, to use Christa Olson's words in *Constitutive Visions* (2014), "they are live analytical terms, charged with the energy of contemporary rhetorical theory" (xix) *and* because the Greco-Latin was part and parcel of the belief systems of the colonizers. They would have been educated in the ways of Aristotle's *Rhetoric*, not only through the medieval scholastics but through the work of Averroës of Córdoba in Andalucía (see Lahcen Elyazghi Ezzarer's *Three Treatises on Aristotle's Rhetoric*, 2015). Even the most sympathetic of the colonizers, Bartolomé de las Casas, argued that since the indigenous of the New World were no less intellectually able than the colonizers, the rhetorical ways of Spain would not need adjustment in being taught (see Don Paul Abbot's *Rhetoric in the New World*, 1996). In other words, the commonplaces of Greco-Roman rhetoric would have been known by the educated among the conquerors and would have been, thereby, among the rhetorical terms that symbolically represented the colonizers' exercise of power.

9. Sources that are not explicitly mentioned in footnotes can be found in the Bibliography.

10. Apart from all figurative language being in some sense metaphorical, I bring up metaphor here because the story that follows the anecdote is based on contemporary studies of the

Yanomami, especially José Antonio Kelly Luciana's "On Yanomami Ceremonial Dialogues: A Political Aesthetic of Metaphorical Agency" in the *Journal de la Societé des Américanistes*, 2017. That said, there is nothing empirical to suggest that the Taíno were descended specifically from the Yanomami. And even as I word-paint a picture of the Bering Straits Journey, I realize that that particular origin story is highly contested, with DNA even suggesting ancient sea travel from Oceania to South America and travels from the indigenous of Africa (an unacknowledged U.S. oversight in labeling Black as other than Indigenous, that Black Africans are African indigenous). In terms of the Taíno, what we do know is that the Taíno traveled to the Caribbean from somewhere along the Orinoco River of South America. Now, some of what is here first appeared in my rendering of "The First 'Indians'" (2010) and was then updated (maybe "corrected" would be the better term) in "Mode Meshing: Before the New World was New" (2020).

11. This comes from Eduardo Galeano's "Origin of Languages" in *Mirrors: Stories of Almost Everyone*, 2009.

12. This is the trope of naming. So many in history have been renamed to Latin and to Spanish and then to English or otherwise Anglicized. And not only persons have been renamed but things, of course. And when the new names for people and things become mandated and a new language is unnecessarily imposed, entire cultures undergo a renaming. This is the path to assimilation, becoming one with the conquerors, losing the self that was.

13. *F* and *Y* were emblazoned on Colón's expeditionary banner, the letters standing for Fernando and Ysabel. Cristoforo Colombo had chosen to change his name to the Castilian *Cristóbal Colón de Carvajal* but certainly not the Anglo-Latin Christopher Columbus, nor would either of the Catholic Monarchs have known or chosen to Anglicize to Ferdinand and Isabella (which is Italian). See "Christopher Columbus' Expeditionary Banner 'La Capitana.'"

14. The words are from Colón's diary of the first voyage, as translated by Kevin Siepel in *Conquistador Voices: The Spanish Conquest of the Americas as Recounted Largely by the Participants*, 2015, 22-23.

15. Siepel, 21-22.

16. It's odd to me that the learned Walter Mignolo would turn to "The Juror of the Third Reich," Carl Schmitt (on page 32 of *Western Modernity*), to make the case for the transition from a theological power ideology to a scientific one. That is a given, not needing Schmitt. But what is more troubling is Mignolo's quoting Schmitt's assertion that before 1500, "the earth was still not measured as a globe," which is simply not true. Plato had attempted a measurement of the world-as-globe, so had Aristotle, and Eratosthenes in 250 BCE not only measured but came mighty close to the current measurement.

17. This translation comes from J.M. Cohen's *The Four Voyages of Christopher Columbus: Being His Own Log-Book, Letters and Dispatches with Connecting Narratives Drawn from the Life of the Admiral by His son Hernando Colon and Other Contemporary Historians*, 1969, 92.

18. This is from the diary of Dr. Álvarez Chanca, 1493, revised by Fray Bartolomé de las Casas, 1527 (in Karl Wagenheim and Olga Jimenez de Wagenheim's *The Puerto Ricans: A Documentary History*, 2006, 3-4).

19. Jorge Estevez's "Origins of the word *Taíno*," 2016.

20. I had thought to invoke Aristotle's fallacy of *accident*, the hasty generalization, as a way to think about racism (as in, "If true for one, then true for all"), but the philosopher Douglas Watson threw a wrench in that by arguing that the very concept of "generalization" is tricky, arguing that there are three different kinds of generalization (in "Rethinking the Fallacy of Hasty Generalization," 1999). Besides, I sure didn't want to get into Aristotelian formal and informal logics, so I thought I'd invoke *synecdoche* as a trope of racism: believing to know the whole based on a part (like knowing all there is to know of a person based on the color of the person's skin). As for *irony*, Bushika will explain that well enough in the chapter.

21. The myths of Hispan or Espan are referred to within the *Historiarum Philippacarum* of Justinus (the first century BCE) according to the "Mitología en la Historiografía Española de la Edad Media y del Ranacimiento" in Robert Brian Tate's *Ensayos Sobre la Historiografía Peninsular del Siglo XV*, 1970.

22. In Amerigo Vespucci's *Mondus Novus Vespucci* of 1504, Vespucci writes to Lorenzo Pietro di Medici, declaring that "these [new regions] we may rightly call a new world." Somehow the phrase caught on, and a few years later, in 1507, the German cartographer Martin Waldeesmüler would ink the name "America" to this new world.

23. I know that I've gotten ahead of myself historically here, but this God-term, to use Kenneth Burke's term in *A Grammar of Motives*, 73, begins here in the late 15th century, early 16th century Europe.

24. Virgil's Eclogue IV.

25. I updated the passage to a more contemporary English (Who says *whither* anymore, for example?), but the passage is drawn from Charles Horne's *Sacred Books and Early Literature of the East*, 241-242.

26. I'm thinking here of the *Illiad*, of course: Odysseus' plea to Achilles in Book IX.

27. This is a paraphrase of a line in Kenneth Burke's "Four Master Tropes" in *A Grammar or Motives*: "True irony, humble irony, is based upon a sense of fundamental kinship with the enemy, as *one needs* him, is *indebted* to him, is not merely outside him as an observer but contains him *within*, being consubstantial with him" (514).

28. This is the trope of *appearing* to concede an argument—appearing, the concession acknowledged as a joke or with contempt (as in "yeah, yeah," clearly not a concession) or the concession that opens a counter or more important argument (as in "yeah, but").

29. Although Alicia is a fiction, the mulatto corsair Miguel Enríquez is a real historical figure though one not discussed in the histories of Puerto Rico until relatively recently. See Angel López Cantos' *Miguel Enríquez: Corsario Boricua del Siglo XVIII*, 1994.

30. This dating back to Ancient Greece comes from Perry Anderson's *The H-Word: The Peripeteia of Hegemony*, 2017, where he writes that "[h]istorically, of course, the origins of the term hegemony are Greek, from a verb meaning to 'guide' or to 'lead,' going back to Homer" and that the "historian [George] Grote—

an associate of John Stuart Mill—argued that *hēgemonia* was leadership freely based on 'attachment or consent,' whereas *arkhē* implied the 'superior authority and coercive dignity' of empire" (1). But rather than this distinction between coercion and consent, Stuart Hall writes that "coercion becomes, as it were, the natural and routine form in which consent is secured," a coercion that does not invoke outright violence but is delivered rhetorically as a "tougher government posture" (in Anderson, 87).

31. See Laura Sook Duncombe's *Pirate Women: The Princesses, Prostitutes, and Privateers Who Ruled the Seven Seas*, 2017.

32. The word *vecino* comes to mean "neighbor." I'm not quite sure what to do with that, in terms of a rhetoric of coloniality.

33. This depiction of race is not always or even generally accepted by Puerto Ricans of the Island (discussed by Marta Cruz-Janzen's "Out of the Closet: Racial Amnesia, Avoidance, and Denial: Racism Among Puerto Ricans" and especially the research of Isar Godreau at the University of Puerto Rico-Cayey). Though it is true that there is a more forgiving attitude about color in Puerto Rico, the real political-economic and other consequences of racism remain in what she calls a *blanqueamiento*, a favoring of whiteness over other racialized differences (see a number of sources in the bibliography).

34. See Jay Richards' "The Economic Thought of Friar Tomás de Mercado: A Dominican Synthesis" in the *Journal of Markets & Morality* (2019), 457-468 and Unisinos Culleton and Alfredo Santiago, "Tomás de Mercado on Slavery: Just According to Law, Unjust in Practice (2015), 29-38.

35. Jane Sutton and Mari Lee Mifsud define *alloiōsis* as the trope meaning "difference, diversity and strangeness" in *A Revolution in Tropes: Alloiostrophic Rhetoric*, 2019, loc. 316 of 42249. Where Sutton and Mifsud invoke this trope to acknowledge these three elements—difference, diversity, and strangeness—to incorporate elements that tend to be systemically excluded within democracy (not just racism but all systemic exclusions), I invoke it here just to mark the differences that emerge as empires shifted in Europe and the Western Hemisphere, altering how difference, diversity, and strangeness are regarded, given changes in power relations and the

attempts to resist the changes. Simply put, I invoke alloiōsis as a trope depicting shifting terms as the colony-that-was became the colony-that-is.

36. This is recorded in Dana Wegner's, "New Interpretations of How the USS Maine Was Lost," in *Theodore Roosevelt, the U.S. Navy, and the Spanish-American War* (2001), 7-17.

37. All of this is explained in my "Puerto Rico: A Neoliberal Crucible" in the *Journal of Cultural Economics*, 2014.

38. Amy Kaplan, *The Anarchy of Empire in the Making of U.S. Culture* (2005), 2.

39. Kaplan, *The Anarchy of Empire*, 6.

40. See Eileen Welsome's *The Plutonium Files: America's Secret Medical Experiments in the Cold War* (2000). Albizu was among thousands of unwitting experimental subjects noted in Nelson Denis's "King of the Towels: The Torture and Murder of Pedro Albizu Campos" (2015).

41. *Time Magazine*, 15 February 1932.

42. I focus a little more closely on Pedro Albizu Campos in "Colonial Memory and the Crime of Rhetoric: Pedro Albizu Campos," *College English* (2009).

43. Boaventura de Sousa Santos rehearses these same limitations and both sides of hegemony (the ideological and the coercive) during the 20th and 21st centuries under the heading "The Limits of Nuestra America" in *Epistemologies of the South*, 64.

44. This is the trope where one repeats what has already been said as a way to move an argument forward.

45. The poem was written by Dad. I found it and other poems in a notebook after his death (where the words even included scansion markings; I had no idea he knew of such things, the stuff I learned in college as an English major). The poems were to Mom, María Socorro Cotto de Villanueva, Soqui. Dad, with an eighth-grade education earned through the GI Bill. Dad, a laborer, a mechanic, and a singer—and a poet! The translation is mine, my own struggle as a "heritage speaker." Soon after I was born, Mom decided that my name would be too long for these Americans, so Víctor Villanueva

y Cotto, the accent penned in, became Victor Villanueva, Jr. and, as a concession to Mom, Dad dropped "y Hernández," his mother's name.

46. From the 1 August 1964 issue of *The New Yorker Magazine*.

47. See Rocío Zambrana's *Colonial Debts: The Case of Puerto Rico*, 2021, especially the Introduction (1-20), for insight into the ways of the young Boricuas of Puerto Rico right now: the young Boricuas who are no longer willing to accommodate.

Bibliography

Abbot, Don Paul. *Rhetoric in the New World: Rhetorical Theory and Practice in Colonial Spanish America.* Columbia, SC: University of South Carolina Press, 1996.

Acharya, Amitav. "Race and Racism in the Founding of the Modern World Order." *International Affairs* 98 no. 1 (2022): 23-43.

Acosta, Ivonne. *La Palabra Como Delito: Los Discursos por los que Condenaron a Pedro Albizu Campos, 1948-1950.* San Juan, PR: Editorial Cultural, 2000.

Altman, Ida. *Life and Society in the Early Spanish Caribbean: The Greater Antilles, 1493-1550.* Baton Rouge: Louisiana State University Press, 2021.

Anderson, Perry. *The H-Word: The Peripeteia of Hegemony.* Brooklyn: Verso, 2017.

Badillo, Jalil Sued. *Agüeybaná el Bravo: la Recuperación de un Símbolo.* San Juan, Puerto Rico: Ediciones Puerto, 2008.

Bonilla-Silva, Eduardo. *Racism without Racists. Color-Blind Racism and the Persistence ofRacial Inequality in America.* New York: Rowman & Littlefield, 2006, 2022.

Boyd-Bowman, Peter. "The Regional Origins of the Earliest Spanish Colonists of America." *PMLA*, vol. 71, no. 5 (1956), 1152-1172.

Brady, Ivan. "The Myth-Eating Man," Review of *The Man-Eating Myth: Anthropology and Anthropophagy* by W. Arens. *American Anthropologist* 84, no. 3 (1982): 595-611.

Burke, Kenneth. *A Grammar of Motives.* Berkeley: University of California Press, 1969.

—. *A Rhetoric of Motives.* Berkeley: University of California Press, 1969.

Charles River Editors. *The Arawak: The History and Legacy of the Indigenous Natives in South America and the Caribbean.* Hingham, MA: Charles River Press, 2019.

Cherwitz, Richard A. and James W. Hikins. *Communication and Knowledge: An Investigation in Rhetorical Epistemology.* Columbia, South Carolina: University of South Carolina Press, 1986.

Civantos, Christina. *The Afterlife of al-Andalus: Muslim Iberia in Contemporary Arab and Hispanic Narratives.* Albany: SUNY Press, 2017.

Cohen, Chaim. "Eden." In *The Oxford Dictionary of the Jewish Religion*, edited by Adele Berlin and Maxine Grossman, Oxford: Oxford University Press, 2011, 228-29.

Cohen, J.M. Editor and translator. *The Four Voyages of Christopher Columbus: Being His Own Log-Book, Letters and Dispatches with Connecting Narratives Drawn from the Life of the Admiral by His son Hernando Colon and Other Contemporary Historians.* London: Penguin Books, 1969.

Cruz-Janzen, Marta I. "Out of the Closet: Racial Amnesia, Avoidance, and Denial: Racism Among Puerto Ricans." *Race, Gender & Class*, vol. 10, no. 3 (2003): 64-81.

Culleton Unisinos, Alfredo Santiago. "Tomás de Mercado on Slavery: Just According to Law, Unjust in Practice. *Patristica et Mediaevalia*, vol. 36 (2015): 29-38.

Curet, L. Antonio. *Caribbean Paleodemography: Population, Culture History, And Sociopolitical Processes in Ancient Puerto Rico.* Tuscaloosa, AL: University of Alabama Press, 2005.

Darity, William A. Jr., Jason Dietrich, Darrick Hamilton. "Bleach in the Rainbow: Latin Ethnicity and Preference for Whiteness." *Transforming Anthropology*, 13 no. 2 (2005): 103-109.

Denis, Nelson A. "King of the Towels: The Torture and Murder of Pedro Albizu Campos." *A Futuro* Media Property, 10 March 2015, https://www.latinorebels.com/2015/03/10/kingof-the-to wels-the-torture-and-murder-of-pedro-albizu-campos/

Diamond, Jared. *Guns, Germs, and Steel.* New York: Norton, 1999.

District of Puerto Rico. "Christopher Columbus' Expeditionary Banner 'La Capitana.'" United States District Court. www.prd.uscourts.gov/christopher-columbus-expeditionary-banner-la-capitana

Duncombe, Laura Sook. *Pirate Women: The Princesses, Prostitutes, and Privateers Who Ruled the Seven Seas.* Chicago: Chicago Review Press, 2017.

Dussel, Enrique. *Philosophy of Liberation.* Eugene, OR: Wipf and Stock, 2003.

—. *The Invention of the Americas: Eclipse of "the Other" and the Myth of Modernity.* Translated by Michael D. Barber. New York: Continuum, 1995.

Ezzaher, Lahcen Elyazghi. Editor and translator. *Three Arabic Treatises on Aristotle's* Rhetoric: *The Commentaries of al-Fārabī, Avicenna, and Averroes.* Carbondale: Southern Illinois University Press, 2015.

Estevez, Jorge. "Origins of the word Taíno" 2016. Accessed January 2, 2021, https://www.researchgate.net/publication/296694496.

Frank, Andre Gunder. *ReOrient: Global Economy in the Asian Age.* Berkeley: University of California Press, 1998.

Galeano, Eduardo. "Origin of Languages." *Mirrors: Stories of Almost Everyone.* Translated by Mark Fried, 42, New York: Nation Books, 2009.

Godreau, Isar P. "Changing Space, Making Race: Distance, Nostalgia, and the Folklorization of Blackness in Puerto Rico. *Identities: Global Studies in Culture and Power* 9, no. 3 (2002): 281-304.

—. "Folkloric 'Others': Blanqueamiento and the Celebration of Blackness as an Exception in Puerto Rico. In *Globalization and Race: Transformations in Cultural Politics of Blackness*, edited by Kamari Maxine Clarke and Deborah A. Thomas, Durham, NC: Duke University Press, 171-187.

Godreau, Isar P. and Carlos Vargas-Ramos. "Which Box Am I?: Towards a Culturally Grounded, Contextually Meaningful

Method of Racial and Ethnic Categorization in Puerto Rico,"
Cuadernos de Investigación 8 (2009): 1-59.

Graetz, Heinrich Hirsch. *History of the Jews.* Vol. 3. Chestnut Hill,
MA: Adamant, 2005.

Greer, Margaret R., Walter D. Mignolo, and Maureen Quilligan,
eds. *Rereading the Black Legend: The Discourses of Religious
and Racial Difference in the Renaissance Empires.* Chicago:
University of Chicago Press, 2007.

Grosfoguel, Ramón. "The Epistemic Decolonial Turn: Beyond
Political-Economy Paradigms," *Cultural Studies* 21, nos. 2-3
(2007): 211-223.

Hall, Edith. *Inventing the Barbarian: Greek Self-Definition Through
Tragedy.* New York: Oxford UP, 1989.

Hannaford, Ivan. *Race: The History of an Idea in the West.* Baltimore:
Johns Hopkins UP, 1996.

Harrington, M.R. *Cuba Before Columbus.* Part I Vol I. New York:
Museum of the American Indian Heye Foundation, 1921.
Google Books.

Homer. *The Illiad.* Translated by Richmond Lattimore. Chicago: The
University of Chicago Press, 2011.

Horne, Charles F., ed. *The Sacred Books and Early Literature of the
East.* New York: Parke, Austin, & Lipscomb, 1917, 241-242.
https://sourcebooks.fordham.edu/source/711tarik1.asp

Hunter, Charlayne. "Comment." *The New Yorker.* August 1, 1964.
https://www.newyorker.com/magazine/1964/08/01/
comment-4933

Jiménez de Wagenheim, Olga. *Puerto Rico: An Interpretive History
from Pre-Columbian Times to 1900.* Princeton: Markus
Wiener, 1998.

—. *Puerto Rico's Revolt for Independence: El Grito de Lares.* Princeton:
Markus Wiener, 1993.

Kaplan, Amy. *The Anarchy of Empire in the Making of U.S. Culture.*
Cambridge, MA: Harvard University Press 2005.

Kelly Luciani, José Antonio. "On Yanomami Ceremonial Dialogues: A Political Aesthetic of Metaphorical Agency." *Journal de la Société des Américanistes* 103 no. 1 (2017): 179-214.

Lehmann, Martin. "The Depiction of America on Martin Waldseemüller's World Map from 1507—Humanistic Geography in the Service of Political Propaganda." *Cogent Arts & Humanities* 3, no. 1 (2016): 1-15.

Lizot, Jacques. *Diccionario Yanomami-Español.* Caracas: Central University of Venezuela, 1975.

Lloréns, Hilda, Carlos G. García-Quijano, Isar P. Godreau. "Racismo en Puerto Rico: Surveying Perceptions of Racism." *Centro Journal* 29 no. 3 (2017): 154-183.

López Cantos, Angel. *Miguel Enríquez: Corsario Boricua del Siglo XVIII.* San Juan, Puerto Rico: Ediciones Puerto, 1994.

Lovén, Sven. *Origins of the Tainan Culture, West Indies.* (Originally published: Géteborg: Elandersboktryckeri aktiebolag, 1935.) Tuscaloosa: The University of Alabama Press, 2010.

Mann, Charles C. *1493: Uncovering the New World Columbus Created.* New York: Vintage Books, 2011.

Matos-Rodríguez, Félix V. and Pedro Juan Hernández. *Pioneros Puerto Ricans in New York City, 1896-1948,* Bilingual Edition. Charleston: Arcadia Publishing, 2001.

Mignolo, Walter D. "Delinking: The Rhetoric of Modernity, the Logic of Coloniality and the Grammar of de-coloniality." *Cultural Studies,* 21 nos. 2-3 (March/May 2007), 449-514.

—. *The Darker Side of Western Modernity: Global Futures, Decolonial Options.* Durham: Duke University Press, 2011.

—. *The Idea of Latin America.* Malden, MA: Blackwell Publishing, 2005.

Mouffe, Chantal. *On the Political.* London: Routledge, 2005.

Olson, Christa J. *Constitutive Visions: Indigeneity and Commonplaces of National Identity in Republican Ecuador.* University Park, PA: The Pennsylvania University Press, 2014.

Owens, J.B. *"By My Absolute Royal Authority": Justice and Castilian Commonwealth at the Beginning of the First Global Age.* Rochester: University of Rochester Press, 2005.

Pimantel, Ryan. *Puerto Rican Vodou: A Brief Introduction to Sanse Religion.* Self-published, 2020.

Polanyi, Michael. *The Tacit Dimension.* Chicago: University of Chicago Press, 1966.

Quijano, Aníbal. "Coloniality and Modernity/Rationality." *Cultural Studies* 21 nos. 2-3 (2007): 168-178.

—. *Ensayos en Torno a la Colonialidad del Poder.* Buenos Aires: Ediciones del Siglo, 2019.

Restall, Matthew. "The Black Conquistadors: Armed Africans in Early Spanish America." *The Americas,* 57 no. 2 (2000): 171-205.

Ribes Tovar, Frederico. *Albizu Campos: Puerto Rican Revolutionary.* New York: Plus Ultra, 1971.

Richards, Jay W. "The Economic Thought of Friar Tomás de Mercado: A Dominican Synthesis." *Journal of Markets & Morality,* 22 no. 2 (2019): 457-468.

Rivera-Rideau, Petra R. "From Carolina to Loíza: Race, Place and Puerto Rican Racial Democracy." *Identities: Global Studies in Culture and Power* 00 no. 00 (2013): 1-17.

Rouse, Irving. *The Tainos: Rise and Decline of the People who Greeted Columbus.* New Haven: Yale University Press, 1992.

Russo, Lucio. *The Forgotten Revolution: How Science Was Born in 300 BC and Why It Had to Be Reborn.* Translated by Silvio Levy. Berlin: Springer, 2004. Kindle

San Juan, Epifanio, Jr. *Racism and Cultural Studies: Critiques of Multiculturalist Ideology and the Politics of Difference.* Durham: Duke University Press, 2002.

Santos, Boaventura de Sousa. *Epistemologies of the South: Justice Against Epistemicide.* New York: Routledge, 2016.

Scott, Robert L. "On Viewing Rhetoric as Epistemic." *Central States Speech Journal* 18, no. 1 (May 1967): 9-17.

Siepel, Kevin H. *Conquistador Voices: The Spanish Conquest of the Americas as Recounted Largely by the Participants*, Vols. 1 & 2. Angola, NY: Spruce Tree Press, 2015.

Snowden, Frank M., Jr. *Blacks in Antiquity: Ethiopians in the Greco-Roman Experience*. Cambridge, MA: Belknap. 1970.

—. *Before Color Prejudice: The Ancient View of Blacks*. Cambridge, MA: Harvard University Press, 1983.

Sutton, Jane S. and Mari Lee Mifsud. *A Revolution in Tropes: Alloiostrophic Rhetoric*. Blue Ridge Summit, PA: Lexington Books, 2019. Kindle.

Tate, Robert B. *Ensayos Sobre la Historiografía Peninsular del Siglo XV*. Madrid: Editorial Gredos, 1970.

Time. "Medicine: Porto Ricochet." February 15, 1932.

Thacher, John Boyd. *Christopher Columbus: His Life, His Work, His Remains, as Revealed by Original Printed and Manuscript Records, Together with an Essay on Peter Martyr of Angbera and Bartolomé de las Casas, the First Historians of America*, Vol. III. New York: The Knickerbocker Press, 1904. Kindle Edition.

Valesio, Paolo. *Novantiqua: Rhetorics as a Contemporary Theory*. Bloomington: Indiana University Press, 1980.

Vander Linden, H. "Alexander VI. And the Demarcation of the Maritime Colonial Domains of Spain and Portugal, 1493-1494." *The American Historical Review* 22 (1916): 1-20.

Vankin, Jonathan and John Whalen. *The Fifty Greatest Conspiracies of All Time: History's Biggest Mysteries, Coverups, and Cabals*. Sacramento, CA: Citadel Press, 1994.

Vespucci, Amerigo. *Mondus Novus: Letter to Lorenzo Pietro di Midici*. 1504. Translated by George Tyler Northrup. Princeton: Princeton University Press, 1916.

Villanueva, Victor. "An Introduction to Social Scientific Discussions on Class." In *Coming To Class: Pedagogy and the Social Class of Teachers* edited by Gary Tate, Alan Shepard, and John McMillan. Portland, ME: Boynton/Cook-Heinemann, 1998, 267-282.

—. *Bootstraps: From an American of Color.* Urbana, IL: National Council of Teachers of English, 1993.

—. "Colonial Memory and the Crime of Rhetoric: Pedro Albizu Campos." *College English* 71, no. 6 (2009), 630-638.

—. "Hegemony: From an Organically Grown Intellectual," *PRE/TEXT: A Journal of Rhetorical Theory* 13 nos. 1-2 (Spring/Summer 1992): 18-34.

—. "Mode Meshing: Before the New World was New." *Talking Back: Senior Scholars Deliberate on the Past, Present, and Future of Writing Studies,* edited by Norbert Elliot and Alice S. Horning. Denver, CO: Utah State University Press, 2020, 343-358.

—. "Puerto Rico: A Neoliberal Crucible. *Journal of Cultural Economy.* DOI: 10.1080/17530350.2014.942348.

—. "The First 'Indians': The Taínos of the Second Voyage of Columbus." *Rhetorics of the Americas: 3114 BCE to 2012 CE.,* edited by Damián Baca and Victor Villanueva, New York: Palgrave Macmillan, 2010, 15-20.

—. "Whose Voice Is It Anyway? Rodriguez' Speech in Retrospect." *The English Journal* 76 no. 8 (December 1987): 17-21.

Virgil. *Eclogues.* Translated by David Ferry. New York: Farrar, Straus and Giroux, 1999.

Wagenheim, Karl and Olga Jimenez de Wegenheim, eds. *The Puerto Ricans: A Documentary History.* Princeton: Markus Wiener, 2006.

Wanzer-Serrano, Darrel. "Decolonial Rhetoric and a Future Yet-to-Become: A Loving Response." *Advances in the History of Rhetoric* 21 no. 3 (2018): 326-330.

Watson, Douglas. "Rethinking the Hasty Generalization." *Argumentation* 13 (May 1999): 161-182.

Wegner, Dana. "New Interpretations of How the *USS Maine* Was Lost." In *Theodore Roosevelt, the U.S. Navy, and the Spanish-American War,* edited by Edward J. Moralda. New York: Palgrave Macmillan, 2001, 7-17.

Welsome, Eileen. *The Plutonium Files: America's Secret Medical Experiments in the Cold War.* El Dorado, Arkansas: Delta Press, 2000.

Wessman, James W. "The Demographic Structure of Slavery in Puerto Rico: Some Aspects of Agrarian Capitalism in the Late Nineteenth Century." *Journal of Latin American Studies* 12 no. 2 (1980): 271–289.

Zack, Naomi. *Philosophy of Race: An Introduction.* London: Palgrave Macmillan, 2018.

Zambrana, Rocío. *Colonial Debts: The Case of Puerto Rico.* Durham: Duke University Press, 2021.

About the Author

Victor Villanueva is Regents Professor and Edward R. Meyer Distinguished Professor of Liberal Arts at Washington State University. He is the author, editor, or co-editor of eight books and nearly fifty articles or chapters in books. Among his books are the award-winning *Bootstraps, From an American Academic of Color, Rhetorics of the Americas: 3114 BCE to 2013 CE*, and *Cross-Talk in Comp Theory: A Reader*, one of the most-adopted books for the training of English teachers of writing in the U.S. and abroad.